New Day

Edited by **Sally Welch**   May–August 2020

The Bible Reading Fellowship
15 The Chambers, Vineyard
Abingdon OX14 3FE
brf.org.uk

The Bible Reading Fellowship (BRF) is a Registered Charity (233280)

ISBN 978 0 85746 904 5
All rights reserved

This edition © The Bible Reading Fellowship 2020
Cover image: Chapel in Bethlehem © iStock.com/jagi11; illustration on page 143
© iStock.com/OllgaP

Distributed in Australia by:
MediaCom Education Inc, PO Box 610, Unley, SA 5061
Tel: 1 800 811 311 | admin@mediacom.org.au

Distributed in New Zealand by:
Scripture Union Wholesale, PO Box 760, Wellington
Tel: 04 385 0421 | suwholesale@clear.net.nz

Acknowledgements

Scripture quotations marked with the following acronyms are taken from the version shown. Where no acronym is given, the quotation is taken from the same version as the headline reference. NRSV: The New Revised Standard Version of the Bible, Anglicised Edition, copyright © 1989, 1995 by the Division of Christian Education of the National Council of the Churches of Christ in the USA. Used by permission. All rights reserved. NIV: The Holy Bible, New International Version, Anglicised edition, copyright © 1979, 1984, 2011 by Biblica. Used by permission of Hodder & Stoughton Publishers, an Hachette UK company. All rights reserved. 'NIV' is a registered trademark of Biblica. UK trademark number 1448790. MSG: *The Message*, copyright © 1993, 1994, 1995, 1996, 2000, 2001, 2002 by Eugene H. Peterson. Used by permission of NavPress. All rights reserved. Represented by Tyndale House Publishers, Inc. BCP: *The Book of Common Prayer*, the rights in which are vested in the Crown, is reproduced by permission of the Crown's Patentee, Cambridge University Press. NEB: The New English Bible (New Testament) © 1961 The Delegates of the Oxford University Press and the Syndics of the Cambridge University Press.

'Daisies are our silver' by Jan Struther (1901–53) from *Enlarged Songs of Praise 1931*. Reproduced by permission of Oxford University Press. All rights reserved.

'O Lord, all the world belongs to you' by Patrick Appleford. Reproduced by permission of Josef Weinberger Ltd.

A catalogue record for this book is available from the British Library

Printed by Gutenberg Press, Tarxien, Malta

Suggestions for using *New Daylight*

Find a regular time and place, if possible, where you can read and pray undisturbed. Before you begin, take time to be still and perhaps use the BRF Prayer on page 6. Then read the Bible passage slowly (try reading it aloud if you find it over-familiar), followed by the comment. You can also use *New Daylight* for group study and discussion, if you prefer.

The prayer or point for reflection can be a starting point for your own meditation and prayer. Many people like to keep a journal to record their thoughts about a Bible passage and items for prayer. In *New Daylight* we also note the Sundays and some special festivals from the church calendar, to keep in step with the Christian year.

New Daylight and the Bible

New Daylight contributors use a range of Bible versions, and you will find a list of the versions used opposite. You are welcome to use your own preferred version alongside the passage printed in the notes. This can be particularly helpful if the Bible text has been abridged.

New Daylight affirms that the whole of the Bible is God's revelation to us, and we should read, reflect on and learn from every part of both Old and New Testaments. Usually the printed comment presents a straightforward 'thought for the day', but sometimes it may also raise questions rather than simply providing answers, as we wrestle with some of the more difficult passages of scripture.

New Daylight is also available in a deluxe edition (larger format). Visit your local Christian bookshop or BRF's online shop **brfonline.org.uk**. To obtain a cassette version for the visually impaired, contact Torch Trust for the Blind, Torch House, Torch Way, Northampton Road, Market Harborough LE16 9HL; +44 (0)1858 438260; **info@torchtrust.org**. For a Braille edition, contact St John's Guild, Sovereign House, 12–14 Warwick Street, Coventry CV5 6ET; +44 (0)24 7671 4241; **info@stjohnsguild.org**.

Comment on *New Daylight*

To send feedback, please email **enquiries@brf.org.uk**, phone **+44 (0)1865 319700** or write to the address shown opposite.

Writers in this issue

Liz Hoare is an ordained Anglican priest and teaches spiritual formation at Wycliffe Hall, Oxford. Her interests lie in the history and literature of Christian spirituality and their connections with today's world.

Lakshmi Jeffreys is the rector of a parish just outside Northampton. She combines this with being a wife, mother, friend, dog-walker, school governor and various other roles, within and beyond the wider church.

Andy John is the bishop of Bangor and has served there for nine years. Apart from being a bishop he occasionally attempts marathons and enjoys time with his now grown-up children.

Geoff Lowson is a retired priest living in a small village in the west of County Durham. In addition to parochial ministry, he spent 21 years working for the mission agency United Society Partners in the Gospel.

Bob Mayo is prison chaplain at HMP Rochester. He has previously been an inner-city youth worker, a university lecturer and a vicar. His publications include research into Generation Y (2006, 2010) and a parish handbook (2016). Bob runs marathons annually.

Ross Moughtin served in the same parish in Liverpool for 26 years, where with his wife Jacqui they led 50 Alpha courses. An international 800-metre runner in his prime, Ross is an enthusiastic member of his local parkrun.

Harry Smart is an Anglican priest and has been mental and general hospital chaplain for many years. He has an interest in mindfulness and in labyrinths and has used them for patient and staff support.

Naomi Starkey is a priest in the Church in Wales, working in Welsh and English across six churches on Anglesey. She was a BRF commissioning editor from 1997 to 2015 and has written a number of books, including *The Recovery of Joy* (BRF, 2017) and *The Recovery of Hope* (BRF, 2016).

Veronica Zundel is an Oxford graduate, writer and columnist. She lives with her husband and son in north London. Her most recent book is *Everything I Know about God, I've Learned from Being a Parent* (BRF, 2013).

Sally Welch writes...

At the time of putting together this issue of *New Daylight*, I am about to lead a pilgrimage to the Holy Land. I have bought a new sunhat, packed plenty of Earl Grey teabags and filled my Kindle with books for the journey. However, I am also making more important preparations – I am re-reading the gospels: reminding myself of the life and ministry of Jesus, mentally matching event to place so that I can help my group enter more fully into the wonderful, transformative experience they are about to engage in.

Obviously you do not have to have visited the places where Jesus lived, preached and healed in order to live a rich Christian life, but even watching a programme or reading a book about this wonderful, troubled land adds an extra dimension to our understanding of the events and challenges that surround the life of Christ. In this issue, Liz Hoare introduces us to the role of Bethlehem and Nazareth, not just in Jesus' times, but drawing on Old Testament events as well to help us understand these complicated towns and the part they play in our faith.

The rest of the issue is not devoid of 'complicated' either – Lakshmi Jeffreys has shown real courage in tackling the tricky topic of the events of Judges 13—21. These chapters not only cover the story of Samson, but also that of Micah, and they are full of the most bloodthirsty and vengeful battles. They show the tragedy that results from a people doing 'what is right in their own eyes' and not following the laws of God. They are an illustration of Paul's declaration, shared by us all, that even though he wants to do right, he still does wrong and leaves the right undone! But Lakshmi also draws profound lessons from these blood-soaked pages, which she sums up as the need of us all for 'the transformative power of the Spirit of God'.

Fortunately, perhaps, we will also read of lighter things – Ross Moughtin explores Matthew 5—7 (the sermon on the mount), and Geoff Lowson shares with us some of his favourite hymns and why he likes them. I hope, too, that my own reflections on pilgrimage and the 'pilgrim heart' will encourage you on your journey through the coming months.

Sally Ann Welch

The BRF Prayer

Almighty God,
you have taught us that your word is a lamp for our feet
and a light for our path. Help us, and all who prayerfully
read your word, to deepen our fellowship with you
and with each other through your love.
And in so doing may we come to know you more fully,
love you more truly, and follow more faithfully
in the steps of your Son Jesus Christ, who lives and reigns
with you and the Holy Spirit, one God forevermore.
Amen

The sermon on the mount

'Help! Someone help me!' A novice surfer was being pulled out to sea by a powerful rip current at Australia's Surfers Paradise. My friend Brian immediately swam towards the panic-stricken swimmer. An experienced surfer himself, he knew what to do. 'Getting the swimmer on to my board was not easy,' he later reflected. 'He was thrashing around, even trying to push me under.'

Once he had the exhausted novice securely on his board, Brian allowed the current to take them even further out to sea and away from the safety of the beach. For Brian knew what the panic-stricken beginner didn't – you don't try to swim against a rip current, otherwise it will soon exhaust you. Only when they were a fair distance away from the beach did Brian raise one arm high out of the water to signal for the lifeguard. In a matter of moments, the lifeguard's rubber dinghy was on the scene and the rescue complete.

Like Brian swimming for safety in apparently the wrong direction, so Jesus summons his disciples to follow him in a completely unexpected direction. Much of what he does makes no sense at the time. We read in Matthew's gospel how the ministry of Jesus begins in Galilee of all places. People would have expected him to make Jerusalem his base, some 70 miles south. That's the first big surprise. There he calls his first disciples, just ordinary fishermen, to follow him. We sense a palpable excitement as his teaching and healings pull in the crowds, and not just from Galilee.

Then at the very outset of his ministry, Jesus gives what we call his sermon on the mount. He takes his disciples aside up on a mountainside to teach them how God works in this world. Much of what he says goes against our deepest instincts: who would love their enemy? Who in their right mind would actually welcome persecution? At the same time, he takes passages from the Old Testament familiar to the disciples and gives them a new, challenging perspective. It's clearly not going to be an easy ride!

To follow Jesus means taking on a totally new way of thinking; the sermon on the mount shows us how to begin to do this.

ROSS MOUGHTIN

Living in God's blessings

'Blessed are the poor in spirit, for theirs is the kingdom of heaven. Blessed are those who mourn, for they will be comforted. Blessed are the meek, for they will inherit the earth. Blessed are those who hunger and thirst for righteousness, for they will be filled. Blessed are the merciful, for they will be shown mercy. Blessed are the pure in heart, for they will see God. Blessed are the peacemakers, for they will be called children of God. Blessed are those who are persecuted because of righteousness, for theirs is the kingdom of heaven.'

Right away Jesus challenges our whole way of thinking with what we call the beatitudes, which means 'blessings'. Each blessing Jesus gives as a simple, memorable phrase. Above all they are good news! God wants to bless us and to bless us richly – an over-the-top, extravagant blessing to the extent that Jesus can say, 'Rejoice and be glad.' It's what our hearts long for; it's where our true happiness lies. But how may we enjoy such blessing?

The big surprise is the kind of people blessed by God. They are the opposite of those we would normally expect, beginning with the poor in spirit and culminating in those who are persecuted because of righteousness. These are the very people, says Jesus, to whom the kingdom of heaven belongs. He uses the present tense to show that, from God's perspective, this is the reality for such people now: theirs is the kingdom of heaven. These two blessings, in framing the whole passage with the same promise, give us the key to understanding the beatitudes. Jesus is teaching about the kingdom of heaven (that is Matthew's way of saying the kingdom of God). And when God is king, everything changes, as he upends the values of this world and welcomes those whom the world disregards.

But we're not there yet. We can see this in the way Jesus uses the future tense for the other blessings in between. They're promises, and we may live today on the basis that God keeps his promises.

Lord, may I listen closely as you teach us how to live today
in the kingdom of heaven.

ROSS MOUGHTIN

Blessed for blessing

'You are the light of the world. A town built on a hill cannot be hidden. Neither do people light a lamp and put it under a bowl. Instead they put it on its stand, and it gives light to everyone in the house. In the same way, let your light shine before others, that they may see your good deeds and glorify your Father in heaven.'

Like a city on a hill or a well-placed lamp, Jesus wants us to stand out, even to be conspicuous. You must shine in such a way, he teaches his disciples, that everyone can see your light. Of course, some people do just 'shine' – you can see it in their faces. I think of Tom, a disciple of many years, who faced bereavement following the death of his wife. Even in his anguish you could see the peace of God shining through his sorrow. Or Ella: again, you could see her total trust in her Lord even as she struggled to respond to a grim diagnosis. Knocked sideways, yes, but not knocked down. Her faith in God's faithfulness was clearly visible for all to see.

Neither Tom nor Ella would have been aware of how much they radiated the light of Christ. They would not have appreciated how much they encouraged others simply by the way they responded to difficult events. Certainly this was not something they had somehow worked up; they would have been only too aware of their weaknesses and failures. But here was God shining through them, his light glowing in a dark place. For Tom and Ella, this was simply through living for God day by day, giving him the opportunity to guide and to guard them in all kinds of situations, allowing him access to every area of their lives. For when we live for Jesus, his light shines, even through us.

So Jesus teaches that we are blessed by God in order to bless others. God's light shines not just in us but through us. His light, not ours. We are the filament through which the Holy Spirit flows.

Lord, show me where I can shine with your light.

ROSS MOUGHTIN

Words which wound and heal

'You have heard that it was said to the people long ago, "You shall not murder, and anyone who murders will be subject to judgement." But I tell you that anyone who is angry with a brother or sister will be subject to judgement. Again, anyone who says to a brother or sister, "Raca," is answerable to the court. And anyone who says, "You fool!" will be in danger of the fire of hell. Therefore, if you are offering your gift at the altar and there remember that your brother or sister has something against you, leave your gift there in front of the altar. First go and be reconciled to them; then come and offer your gift.'

We've all been hurt by a single word from a friend or colleague – 'Raca, you fool!' Such words can cut deep, however much we may try to pretend otherwise. As a vicar, I was often hurt by a sharp word, sometimes unintentionally. These words, with their capacity to wound, Jesus teaches, are in the same category as murder. For murder is much more than you would think, he explains. It includes any way in which we may deliberately hurt each other. For all our actions, even a few hasty words, we are accountable to God.

But then again, we've all been deeply touched by another word – 'sorry'. That single word, too, can make all the difference. So important is this word that we must go to great lengths to say it, even if it means a round trip of 140 miles. To make a gift to God at his altar would have been a very significant event for any of Jesus' listeners. It would mean travelling, usually by foot, from where they were in Galilee to the temple in Jerusalem, some 70 miles distant – with the final 15 miles an uphill slog. Even so, says Jesus, if you are about to offer your gift and realise you need to make up with someone back at home, this has the priority. We are told to keep God waiting while we sort out our relationships back home.

Such is the importance of restoring damaged relationships; such their priority.

Father, show me where I need to make amends
and give me courage to do so.

ROSS MOUGHTIN

Just like your Father

'You have heard that it was said, "Love your neighbour and hate your enemy." But I tell you, love your enemies and pray for those who persecute you, that you may be children of your Father in heaven. He causes his sun to rise on the evil and the good, and sends rain on the righteous and the unrighteous. If you love those who love you, what reward will you get? Are not even the tax collectors doing that? And if you greet only your own people, what are you doing more than others? Do not even pagans do that? Be perfect, therefore, as your heavenly Father is perfect.'

To the amusement of my family, I am turning out to be just like my father. Like him I enjoy all things railway, appreciate the music of Ravel and am doomed to follow Everton FC. Even more, I am beginning to look like him, especially if I wear the flat cap my daughter bought for me for that very reason! During my formative years, I saw how my father lived; I observed what was important to him. Gradually his enthusiasms became mine. My father was not simply my inspiration but also my pattern. I wanted to be like him.

That's the Christian life, says Jesus. As we daily follow him, we develop more of the family likeness. Living our lives for God, we begin to resemble our heavenly Father. Amazing!

Above all, this is to be seen in our relationships, especially with those whom we find difficult. It's one thing loving those who love us; anyone can do that, as Jesus points out. It's something else altogether when we decide to love our enemies, those people who are giving us a tough time. That's the test.

This is God: he cares for all people, including those who oppose him; his blessings flow freely for everyone, even if they do not realise it. Hold on to this, says Jesus. You are a child of God, beloved and special. So show the family likeness. Become the person you already are as his disciple. Be like your Father.

Father, thank you that as your beloved child,
I am showing the family likeness.

ROSS MOUGHTIN

Poised in prayer

'This, then, is how you should pray: "Our Father in heaven, hallowed be your name, your kingdom come, your will be done, on earth as it is in heaven. Give us today our daily bread. And forgive us our debts, as we also have forgiven our debtors. And lead us not into temptation, but deliver us from the evil one."'

As we follow Jesus, prayer is to be at the centre of our lives. In Matthew's gospel, structure is important, and here there's a well-crafted balance with the Lord's Prayer right in the middle of the sermon on the mount. It's as if Matthew is saying that to live a life of poise, you need to live a life of prayer. To maintain your balance, pray to God as your heavenly Father.

We all find prayer both difficult and easy. It comes naturally, and yet we are so easily distracted. So Jesus teaches his disciples how we should pray. His main message is obvious. This prayer is short, very short. We are to resist the temptation of thinking that the longer the prayer, the more likely it is that God is going to respond. Long prayers can so easily feed our egos.

It's short because of who God is. Jesus invites us to call him 'Abba'. Matthew uses the original Aramaic word for 'father', revealing a close, intimate relationship. Above all, our Father loves us and wants the very best for us. So Jesus wants us to pray to God just in the same way we would speak to our earthly father – simply and to the point. Certainly, there is no need for repetition or elaborate phrases.

Above all, the Lord's Prayer is God-centred. We begin with his name, his kingdom. We are to rely on him in the same way that a child would rely on their parent day by day. As always for Jesus, relationship is central. We are to live as God's family, so we are to forgive all those who have wronged us, no exceptions. That's how our heavenly Father wants his children to live, safe in his care.

Ponder the privilege of addressing God as Abba.

ROSS MOUGHTIN

See that plank!

'Do not judge, or you too will be judged. For in the same way as you judge others, you will be judged, and with the measure you use, it will be measured to you. Why do you look at the speck of sawdust in your brother's eye and pay no attention to the plank in your own eye? How can you say to your brother, "Let me take the speck out of your eye," when all the time there is a plank in your own eye? You hypocrite, first take the plank out of your own eye, and then you will see clearly to remove the speck from your brother's eye.'

Have you heard the one about the man with a plank in his eye? A member of my family – I'd better not say which one – always laughs three times when I tell her a joke: first when she hears it, then when I explain it to her and finally when she gets it!

Jesus often used humour in his teaching, such as the use of ridiculous exaggeration. It's a way of getting past our defences, so that as we suddenly get it, we realise that we are laughing at ourselves. Of course, some people take longer than others. Jesus explains that those measures we use to judge or evaluate other people will be the very same ones used to evaluate us. If you are hard on others, expect the same for yourself. You can't have it both ways.

It is so easy to judge other people, finding fault in their lives while being completely oblivious to our own faults. The problem with having a plank in our eye is that we may not be able to see it is there. This huge blind spot may be obvious to others but not to us. Complete honesty and being open to others, especially those who love us, is the key. But also, are we able to laugh at ourselves? Only then are we able to effectively help other people.

Are you hard on other people? What does this tell you about yourself?

ROSS MOUGHTIN

Keep at it

'Ask and it will be given to you; seek and you will find; knock and the door will be opened to you. For everyone who asks receives; the one who seeks finds; and to the one who knocks, the door will be opened. Which of you, if your son asks for bread, will give him a stone? Or if he asks for a fish, will give him a snake? If you, then, though you are evil, know how to give good gifts to your children, how much more will your Father in heaven give good gifts to those who ask him!'

'Mum/Dad, please may I have…' This is a familiar phrase to parents, for asking is what children do. They ask because they depend on us. However, sometimes they just keep on asking and refuse to give up until we give in! This persistence shows that they are confident of our love, if not of our attention span. It would be very different if they thought we were cold or remote.

At the heart of the Christian life is our dependency on God. Jesus teaches that we may rely on God in the same way that a child relies on their parent. But what kind of parent is our heavenly Father?

We learn that he is a Father who loves to give, who enjoys blessing his children. It is not that we have to tiptoe into his study, grit our teeth and tentatively submit our application, knowing that at any time we could be put in our place. No, says Jesus: the very opposite. Just think of how you enjoy giving to your children. No way are you going to give them anything that would hurt them. You want their very best. 'How much more,' Jesus insists, 'will your Father in heaven give good gifts to those who ask him!' This gives us the confidence to keep on asking, to keep on seeking, to keep on knocking. This may seem to us presumptuous, taking advantage of God's compassion. But Jesus encourages us to keep at it – God will never do anything that would spoil us in any way.

What request of your heavenly Father do you need to persevere with?

ROSS MOUGHTIN

Check your bearings

'Enter through the narrow gate. For wide is the gate and broad is the road that leads to destruction, and many enter through it. But small is the gate and narrow the road that leads to life, and only a few find it.'

My wife will tell you that however clear the instructions are in our walking guidebook, I will invariably get lost. However, after years of going astray, I now realise that my main challenge is right at the start of the walk – to take the correct exit out of the car park. The dangerous approach is to follow everyone else. I assume that they are doing the same walk as me. It's so easy to head through the main exit and along the obvious path with everyone else while not seeing the tiny gate behind the bushes on the other side of the car park. So right at the very start of the walk, I need to pause and take time to check out our surroundings, work out where we are and find the correct exit.

In teaching about the kingdom of heaven, Jesus reminds us that we have a similar choice to make. He warns us against following everyone else through the wide gate and along the broad road. Instead, the path to life is narrow and the right gate is small. Jesus is emphasising that this is a crucial decision for each of us to make as individuals. No one can make it for us, and it's a choice we have to make if we are to enter the kingdom of heaven. There is simply no alternative.

The road to life is narrow. We may well find ourselves, if not alone, then walking in single file. And to walk along a narrow path, I know from experience, takes concentration. Moreover, Jesus teaches, there will not be many of us; only a few will find the right path.

Take time out to check your bearings. Have you entered by the small gate? Are you walking along the narrow road to life?

ROSS MOUGHTIN

Firm foundations

'Therefore everyone who hears these words of mine and puts them into practice is like a wise man who built his house on the rock. The rain came down, the streams rose, and the winds blew and beat against that house; yet it did not fall, because it had its foundation on the rock. But everyone who hears these words of mine and does not put them into practice is like a foolish man who built his house on sand. The rain came down, the streams rose, and the winds blew and beat against that house, and it fell with a great crash.'

Crash! Jesus finishes his sermon with the spectacular image of a house crashing down during a storm. Its foundations fail because it is foolishly built on sand. That's what will happen, he warns, if you listen to his words but don't act on them.

How often do we talk with someone and know that they are not listening? You can see it in their faces. They nod, but our words just go in one ear and out the other. It happens all the time in my family: 'Dad, you are just not listening!' my daughters complain. It's easy to not listen, to be preoccupied with our own thoughts. Sometimes we just don't want to hear, as it may mean that we have to change. That's the problem: we can listen to Jesus, even understand what he is saying, but then continue as before. His words have had no impact. We are building on sand.

So how do we listen to Jesus? It is like laying good foundations for a house, even building on rock. It's hard work, far harder than excavating sand, but it's a necessary investment for testing times ahead. At its most basic, to respond to Jesus means deciding to entrust our entire lives to God, whom we may know as our loving heavenly Father. His promises are our rock upon which we may build so that we do not fear the storm, however powerful. Only then do we know the blessings of the kingdom of heaven.

Lord, give me the courage to put your words into practice this day.

ROSS MOUGHTIN

Trees

When I conceived the somewhat eccentric idea of writing on trees in the Bible, I thought that the notes would at most supply a week of readings. After researching the subject, however, I think I could easily have written much more!

I should not have been surprised. Trees are at the heart of the Bible's message. They symbolise spiritual fruitfulness. They are the basis of parables. They are part of the 'wealth' of Israel and other surrounding nations. They stand for security and home, each family sitting under the shade of their own tree. A large range of trees native to the Middle East are mentioned repeatedly, including oak, olive, fig and cedar. (In the famous Russian icon of the Trinity by Andrei Rublev, the oaks of Mamre, where Abraham received his mysterious angelic visitors, are a prominent feature.) The ancients knew, as science has confirmed today, that trees are crucial to the balance of the natural environment. And the whole Bible is framed by the tree of life in Eden at the beginning and its reappearance in the New Jerusalem in Revelation at the end.

I should also not have been surprised, therefore, that writing on biblical trees would lead me into writing on environmental issues and on the morality of war. In an age when the whole future of our planet is under threat, trees are political, and we need political and economic decisions to preserve their vital role in our life on earth. I make no apology for this emphasis; I think it was Desmond Tutu who remarked that when he heard people say the Bible should be kept separate from politics, he wondered what Bible they were reading. The question of who wields power over people and nature is a central theme of our scriptures, from the garden of Eden to the teaching of Jesus. And it's amazing what trees can teach us about this vital issue.

VERONICA ZUNDEL

All we need

So God created humankind in his image, in the image of God he created them; male and female he created them. God blessed them, and God said to them, 'Be fruitful and multiply, and fill the earth and subdue it; and have dominion over the fish of the sea and over the birds of the air and over every living thing that moves upon the earth.' God said, 'See, I have given you every plant yielding seed that is upon the face of all the earth, and every tree with seed in its fruit; you shall have them for food.'

Plant-based diets are all the rage at the moment, for both health and environmental reasons. I have never heard this preached on, but the picture of 'original blessing' that we get in the first two chapters of Genesis is one in which humans, at least, live on a vegetarian or even vegan diet. As Ecclesiastes says, 'there is nothing new under the sun'!

Whether or not you think Christians should imitate this, the overall message is that God has provided in abundance for our physical needs. Our culture often gives us a message of scarcity: resources have to be carefully managed, and what one has, another must go without. But, in fact, there is plenty of food produced in our world, enough to feed every-one adequately at our present population. The trouble is that it is unfairly distributed, and huge amounts are wasted. Ironically, when people are economically secure, their population growth slows – so promoting food justice actually makes it easier, not harder, to feed the world.

Trees are, of course, also vital to balance our ecology; they are a natu-ral carbon-capture mechanism, reversing the greenhouse effect that leads to catastrophic global warming. Yet all the time, rainforests are being cut down to feed the west's greed for products with soya or palm oil. We need to hear the urgent call to save our planet.

The story goes that Luther was asked what he would do if he heard the world was going to end tomorrow. He replied, 'I would plant a tree.' The promise of Jesus' return should make us care for the earth more, not less.

VERONICA ZUNDEL

Exiled from Eden

Then the Lord God said, 'See, the man has become like one of us, knowing good and evil; and now, he might reach out his hand and take also from the tree of life, and eat, and live forever' – therefore the Lord God sent him forth from the garden of Eden, to till the ground from which he was taken. He drove out the man; and at the east of the garden of Eden he placed the cherubim, and a sword flaming and turning to guard the way to the tree of life.

Recently I was looking round a building with a sign on the inside of its heavy door, saying, 'Do not touch this bolt.' What did I immediately want to do? Touch the bolt! I didn't, but it reminded me how, as soon as we humans encounter a prohibition, something in us wants to break it.

The story of Eden is an ancient, mysterious tale. I think it tells us something about the ambivalence of being human. Adam and Eve know only good, and you would think that would be enough. But, deceived into thinking that God is withholding something from them, they seek to be 'like God', knowing evil as well. (In reality, they are already 'in the image of God', so they are as like God as it is possible for humans to be.) Ironically, when they disobey God's command, they become less like God, because they do not have God's capacity to always choose the good.

Why does God then deny them the tree of life? To live forever with a broken relationship to God and the world would be less than the best God has for us – which is to live forever in a restored relationship, through Christ.

Trees as a symbol of the origin of life are a common religious symbol, especially in stories that attempt to explain where we come from. Some of this symbol's power comes from how trees act as a link between earth and 'heaven': their roots in the soil, their branches in the sky. They point us to the thought that God has better plans for our eternal flourishing.

Is there something you feel God is keeping from you?
Talk to God about this feeling.

VERONICA ZUNDEL

Protecting the trees

If you besiege a town for a long time, making war against it in order to take it, you must not destroy its trees by wielding an axe against them. Although you may take food from them, you must not cut them down. Are trees in the field human beings that they should come under siege from you? You may destroy only the trees that you know do not produce food; you may cut them down for use in building siege-works against the town that makes war with you, until it falls.

Deforestation is nothing new. Where I live in north London, there are three primeval woodlands, all that remains of the forest that once covered the whole area. Now they are protected as areas for recreation and environmental conservation.

Humans need, of course, to clear land for agriculture and dwellings. But sometimes war creates unwarranted environmental devastation. If you have seen the artist Paul Nash's paintings of miles of blasted trees after what was then called the Great War, you will have a mental image of how desolate a war-torn landscape can be. Conflict can destroy not just people but also the earth we depend on.

The good news is that the land can recover quickly after this destruction. Within a few years of the armistice, the trees grew again and today, if you visit the battlefields, there is no outward sign of the horrors that went on there (although bones and bullets are still being found 100 years later). God has designed the earth with an inbuilt capacity for renewal.

This should not, however, make us complacent. A nuclear war could kill all life on earth; the destruction at Hiroshima and Nagasaki was a magnitude greater than that at the Somme or Passchendaele, and the world's current nuclear armoury is capable of thousands of Hiroshimas. So it is interesting that God, through Moses, provides a warning against letting war impact our environment too much. This law is as relevant today as it was thousands of years ago.

Pray that the world, from individuals to nations, will learn
'the things that make for peace' (Luke 19:42).

VERONICA ZUNDEL

Be like a tree

Happy are those who do not follow the advice of the wicked, or take the path that sinners tread, or sit in the seat of scoffers; but their delight is in the law of the Lord, and on his law they meditate day and night. They are like trees planted by streams of water, which yield their fruit in its season, and their leaves do not wither. In all that they do, they prosper.

Have you seen those memes on social media that feature a cartoon character, let's call him Bob, whose good characteristics are listed, followed by the punchline 'Be more like Bob'? I have never yet seen one that portrays a tree and says, 'Be more like a tree.' But it's not bad advice.

Trees cannot choose where they are planted, but the good gardener, farmer or forester plants them where they will flourish best: near a source of water, in fertile soil and preferably in a position that receives sunlight. Seeds that fall in the wrong place will simply not germinate, or if they do, their saplings may die or be eaten by animals.

Human beings, on the other hand, have a certain amount of choice. We may not have chosen where we are 'planted', but we can seek out metaphorical water and sunlight in the form of a church that nourishes us, regular retreats, spiritual reading and a discipline of prayer – not to mention friends who build us up rather than tear us down. Psalm 1 advises us to associate with those who have the same values and goals as us; this does not mean we shun others who do not share them, but we do well not to take those others as our role models.

If we follow this advice, the psalm promises us 'fruit in its season', as well as leaves that do not wither. It does not promise constant fruit: there may be periods in our lives when we are putting down roots rather than yielding results. But there will be fruit at the right time, and the leaves – the means by which we grow and take in spiritual nutrition – will keep doing their job.

Where do you find your spiritual nourishment?
Can you make more and better use of this?

VERONICA ZUNDEL

The unkindest cut?

For there is hope for a tree, if it is cut down, that it will sprout again, and that its shoots will not cease. Though its root grows old in the earth, and its stump dies in the ground, yet at the scent of water it will bud and put forth branches like a young plant...

Then [Jesus] told this parable: 'A man had a fig tree planted in his vineyard; and he came looking for fruit on it and found none. So he said to the gardener, "See here! For three years I have come looking for fruit on this fig tree, and still I find none. Cut it down! Why should it be wasting the soil?" He replied, "Sir, let it alone for one more year, until I dig around it and put manure on it. If it bears fruit next year, well and good; but if not, you can cut it down."'

In 2001, when I had breast cancer for the first time, the second reading for today meant a lot to me. It felt as though, to help me bear fruit, God was dumping a lot of 'manure' on me! In the last two years I have revisited that experience. Both of today's passages admit that trees (and people) may endure suffering or barrenness in their lives; but they also tell us that this is not necessarily the end of fruitfulness.

In my local woodlands, the rangers periodically cut the trees down to their base to produce new shoots, a practice known as coppicing. Meanwhile the trees adorning our streets are regularly pollarded, cut back at the top, to promote thicker growth and keep the tree at a manageable height. I'm sure you can work out the parallels with human experience for yourselves. Perhaps the most important lesson is that when we face trials in our lives, rather than assuming they must be a sign of lack of faith or unconfessed sin, we should recognise the effects of living in a damaged world. But it can also be God's means of training us to be more mature and productive disciples of Christ.

Elizabeth Goudge's novel The Scent of Water *(1963) uses a phrase from the first of today's readings to tell the story of a woman with recurrent mental illness. Pray for all who struggle with their mental health.*

VERONICA ZUNDEL

Roots

Christ redeemed us from the curse of the law by becoming a curse for us – for it is written, 'Cursed is everyone who hangs on a tree' – in order that in Christ Jesus the blessing of Abraham might come to the Gentiles, so that we might receive the promise of the Spirit through faith…

But if some of the branches were broken off, and you, a wild olive shoot, were grafted in their place to share the rich root of the olive tree, do not vaunt yourselves over the branches. If you do vaunt yourselves, remember that it is not you that support the root, but the root that supports you.

In the Hebrew scriptures, God's people are often compared to a fig tree or an olive tree, and Jesus takes up these images when he confronts the failures of his people. Paul, too, as a faithful Jew, uses the image of trees to assert that Gentiles who follow Jesus are not a replacement for the original chosen people, the Jews. Rather they are a 'wild olive shoot' that has been grafted into the original stock, sharing in all the blessings promised to the Jewish people – including the blessing of declaring and demonstrating God's ways to the rest of the world.

The fact that the church soon lost touch with its Jewish roots is one of its great historic tragedies (and, centuries later, profoundly influenced the events of the Holocaust). Believers who have come to faith in Jesus from a Jewish background know how much the traditions, festivals and attitudes of their heritage can enrich and inform their new faith. Judaism has much to offer Christianity in its emphasis on living out faith in the home, its more holistic view of the relationship between soul and body, and even its ability to find hope and humour in the darkest of circumstances. As a Jew by birth, I found it a blessing that my Mennonite church used to hold a Passover meal every year. We may need to rediscover these roots and let them inform our life as followers of a Jewish redeemer.

What difference might it make to you (and your church) to think of yourself as grafted into the people God had already chosen?

VERONICA ZUNDEL

Tree of healing

Nation shall not lift up sword against nation, neither shall they learn war any more; but they shall all sit under their own vines and under their own fig trees, and no one shall make them afraid; for the mouth of the Lord of hosts has spoken…

Then the angel showed me the river of the water of life, bright as crystal, flowing from the throne of God and of the Lamb through the middle of the street of the city. On either side of the river is the tree of life with its twelve kinds of fruit, producing its fruit each month; and the leaves of the tree are for the healing of the nations. Nothing accursed will be found there any more.

As I write today, Westminster Abbey is holding a service to celebrate 50 years of Britain's nuclear deterrent. At the same time, Christian peace activists are holding a 'die-in' outside the Abbey to protest against what they see as a celebration of the threat to kill millions of innocent civilians.

Whatever you think about nuclear arms and their morality or effectiveness (and Christians do disagree about issues to do with war), we cannot as Christians deny that the trajectory of the Bible is towards a world free of armaments and the threat of war. There are no weapons of any kind in the new heavens and new earth promised by the scriptures. Instead, Micah portrays a world where it is no longer seen as necessary to 'study war', as the spiritual puts it, but where each family lives in peace under their own fruit-bearing vines and trees. In Micah's vision, trees are not cut down for bows and arrows, siege engines and warships, but only for housing, furniture and art.

Recently, for a hymn-writing competition I wrote a hymn that described the new world God has promised us, with the refrain, 'Why can't we start it now?' I didn't win, but I still think it's a fair question. If God is introducing a kingdom of peace, and we are the first fruits of that kingdom, shouldn't we be working for peace now?

The tree of life is a tree of peace. Pray for those who have the power to foster peace in the world.

VERONICA ZUNDEL

Bethlehem and Nazareth

Geography shapes human life. It always has. Rural or urban, desert or riverside, mountain or plain. The landscape of the Middle East, along with its weather, vegetation and way of life that emerged out of its resources, helped to form Jesus into the person he was. It influenced his parentage, gave him his culture and provided pictures and imagery for his parables and teaching. It had shaped the religion of the people of the land from the beginning and influenced its politics.

We all know the stories associated with Bethlehem and Nazareth, or we think we do. The more familiar we are with stories, the harder it is to see something new. It is also more of a challenge to experience their impact on our lives today as if we were hearing them for the first time. The roles played by Bethlehem and Nazareth as contexts in the unfolding will of God enrich our understanding of Jesus taking on our flesh and how that speaks to us in our context today.

There are problems with locating events precisely. After the Emperor Constantine's mother, Helena, visited the Holy Land in the fourth century and gave her blessing to a number of holy sites, a basilica was erected to mark the link with Jesus. Ever since, Bethlehem and Nazareth have been destinations for countless pilgrims, but what they see in each place often runs counter to expectations. That very shock, however, offers potential for fresh insight into living out the gospel today.

Bethlehem and Nazareth are living towns, where ordinary people continue to live and work, and in many cases struggle with poverty and insecurity. What difference does it make that Jesus once walked here? Even with all their religious paraphernalia, noise and confusion, people are moved as they recall the story of Jesus' birth and realise afresh that God came and pitched his tent among us. Bethlehem and Nazareth remind us that God loved the world so much that he became a human being, experiencing what it is like to be born, grow up and live in this world. Whatever we experience, he has gone before us, even dying a human death. The difference is that he is also risen and is with us now, in every part of life.

LIZ HOARE

Bethlehem: hospitality to strangers

When [Ruth and Naomi] came to Bethlehem, the whole town was stirred because of them; and the women said, 'Is this Naomi?' She said to them, 'Call me no longer Naomi, call me Mara, for the Almighty has dealt bitterly with me. I went away full, but the Lord has brought me back empty; why call me Naomi when the Lord has dealt harshly with me, and the Almighty has brought calamity upon me?' So Naomi returned together with Ruth the Moabite, her daughter-in-law, who came back with her from the country of Moab. They came to Bethlehem at the beginning of the barley harvest.

Feeling a bit lost in a strange city abroad recently, I got chatting to the man behind the counter who served me my pizza. He came from Guyana and had been hounded from two different countries before he found a welcome in the third. He was full of praise for the generous hospitality he had received and the job he had making pizzas every day. In our passage today Naomi was going home, but Ruth had no assurance that she would be welcomed alongside her mother-in-law. Yet she insisted on accompanying her, saying, 'Your people shall be my people, and your God my God. Where you die, I will die – and there will I be buried' (Ruth 1:16–17).

The book of Ruth is a beautifully crafted love story, but it carries much greater significance still, for in the happy outcome Ruth becomes the grandmother of the future king David and the ancestor of the Messiah himself. Ruth, a Gentile, is included as one of four women in Matthew's genealogy of Joseph. Ruth was a Moabite woman, who became a daughter of Bethlehem. It says a great deal for the open-minded generosity of Bethlehem and its inhabitants that she was accepted, but in turn, by making her home there and fulfilling her commitment made to Naomi, she ensured that Bethlehem would be marked out for all time.

Where have you received open-minded generosity recently? Is there a way you and your church could show such generosity to strangers?

LIZ HOARE

Bethlehem: a place to worship

When [the magi] saw that the star had stopped, they were over-whelmed with joy. On entering the house, they saw the child with Mary his mother; and they knelt down and paid him homage. Then, opening their treasure-chests, they offered him gifts of gold, frankincense and myrrh. And having been warned in a dream not to return to Herod, they left for their own country by another road.

If you visit Bethlehem today, you have to stoop to enter the Church of the Nativity. The door was narrowed first by crusaders and again in the time of the Mamluk or Turkish overlords to prevent looters driving carts into the church. It is both a witness to the troubles that Bethlehem has experienced over and over again since biblical times and a symbol of the stance we are invited to adopt before the throne of God incarnate.

Even more than the shepherds who 'saw' and made known all that had happened (Luke 2:15–20), the magi recognised the significance of this child and knelt down and paid him homage. Perhaps it was because they were used to majesty at home and knew a king when they saw one. Perhaps it was the fruit of the long journey they had made and the sign in the heavens which they had studied. They certainly knew that they had made a mistake by going to Herod's palace, so were learning to look in the 'wrong' places for God's activities rather than what they assumed to be the 'right' ones.

Bethlehem had probably never witnessed such wealth all in one place: gold, frankincense and myrrh were exotic and supremely valuable and not normally found in the sort of humble abode where this little family now resided. Did the magi wear their courtly finery, as depicted in the many paintings of this scene? Or did they stay in their travelling gear with a come-as-you-are attitude? What mattered was their homage and the difference it made to them thereafter. Every part of the story invites our wonder, our humility and our adoration.

O come let us adore him, Christ the Lord. Amen

LIZ HOARE

Bethlehem: the house of bread

But you, O Bethlehem of Ephrathah, who are one of the little clans of Judah, from you shall come forth for me one who is to rule in Israel, whose origin is from of old, from ancient days.

If we were drawing up plans for a future of glorious prosperity and peace, we would most likely expect someone with good credentials to take charge. They would originate in some grand metropolis, have attended the right school and move in the best networks. They would be at ease among the rich and powerful, commanding wealth and status of their own.

Not so in God's economy. In the midst of the dreadful condemnation he was called to proclaim, the prophet Micah announces that a ruler will come out of a poor little town six miles south of Jerusalem. Its great claim to fame was that David, Israel's greatest king, was born there, but he chose to make his capital not in his hometown but in nearby Jerusalem.

Dig a little deeper, however, and we find other significant things about Bethlehem. It was the burial place of Rachel, Jacob's beloved wife who died in childbirth (Genesis 35:19) and the setting for much of the story of Ruth and Boaz, David's ancestors. Its name means 'house of bread', and with a name like that Bethlehem begins to make sense.

The prophet Micah, a contemporary of Amos, Hosea and Isaiah, denounced the cities of Samaria and Jerusalem for their dishonest and oppressive practices and their sham religion, but he also had words of hope for a different future. Key to this hope is the ruler who will come, like David of old, from Bethlehem. There is a strong indication – in the reference to his origin 'from of old, from ancient days' – that he will be altogether different from any earthly ruler. Coupled with his earthly birthplace being 'the house of bread' and the associations with David, who was a man after God's heart (see Acts 13:22), we begin to realise that Micah's vision rested on something startlingly new and different. God's plans for his people would not resemble anything dreamed up by humans.

Lord, open our eyes to see your ways and give us grace
to embrace your values. Amen

LIZ HOARE

Sorrow in Bethlehem

When Herod saw that he had been tricked by the wise men, he was infuriated, and he sent and killed all the children in and around Bethlehem who were two years old or under, according to the time that he had learned from the wise men. Then was fulfilled what had been spoken by the prophet Jeremiah: 'A voice heard in Ramah, wailing and loud lamentation, Rachel weeping for her children; she refused to be consoled, because they are no more.'

This is a terrible story in every way. No wonder it does not feature in nativity plays or on Christmas cards. We want Bethlehem to remain picturesque, safe and comforting, the birthplace of the baby Jesus. The Messiah did not come because the world was a happy place, however, but because the world needs saving. Violence, pain and suffering occur in every age, and today the Middle East remains a region of tension, recent wars and cruel suffering. Bethlehem is no stranger to all this, and its hideous dividing wall is testimony to the world's continued captivity to fear, suspicion and rage.

Visitors today are taken to see Banksy's murals covering parts of the wall, which declare defiance and point towards hope through resistance to the dehumanising effects of violence and division. There are also comments and stories of oppression and unfair treatment documented there, often penned by young people. Rachel still weeps for her lost children and finds no comfort.

Herod clung on to his throne, an insecure, power-hungry ruler who could brook no potential rival, even if that rival was a helpless baby. Jesus' life began and ended in violence, and Bethlehem was not immune to it, then or now. Yet there remain signs of hope, even in a striking mural on a symbol of division and hatred. Jesus our Saviour was the subject of suffering and hope too. As the place where the incarnation occurred, Bethlehem signifies these twin aspects of all human life.

Lord Jesus, you are no stranger to our sufferings.
Be with all those who weep for their lost or suffering children
in Bethlehem and throughout the world. Amen

LIZ HOARE

29

Bethlehem: home of kings

The Lord said to Samuel, 'How long will you grieve over Saul? I have rejected him from being king over Israel. Fill your horn with oil and set out; I will send you to Jesse the Bethlehemite, for I have provided for myself a king among his sons.' Samuel said, 'How can I go? If Saul hears of it, he will kill me.' And the Lord said, 'Take a heifer with you, and say, "I have come to sacrifice to the Lord." Invite Jesse to the sacrifice, and I will show you what you shall do; and you shall anoint for me the one whom I name to you.'

Christians associate Bethlehem so strongly with Jesus that we are apt to forget that it has a much longer history. This includes the tangled story of Israel's desire for a king and the abject failure of Saul, which led to God's command to Samuel to seek a new king for Israel, in Bethlehem of all places. Why Bethlehem? God seems to choose the least and the most insignificant of people and places to fulfil his purposes.

Jesse's claim to fame was that he was a man with many sons, and it took some false starts before David was brought before Samuel. He was not even considered important by his family. The last and youngest son, David was out in the fields, looking after sheep. That in itself should make us open our eyes. Over and over again, God surprises us, yet provides us with clues as to what he is up to. Here is a shepherd, learning to care for the weak and the vulnerable, gaining skills that would lead him to true greatness in God's sight. Bethlehem, which had welcomed David's ancestor Ruth, now gave back to the whole of Israel a gift of unsurpassed worth. Its greatest son David rose to be the greatest of Israel's kings, a man after God's own heart.

But there was more. Jesus' followers came to see him as another David, yet one so much greater. Bethlehem was the birthplace of another saviour, not just of Israel but of the whole world.

Lord Jesus Christ, Saviour of the world, grant us your peace.

LIZ HOARE

Back to their roots in Bethlehem

In those days a decree went out from Emperor Augustus that all the world should be registered. This was the first registration and was taken while Quirinius was governor of Syria. All went to their own towns to be registered. Joseph also went from the town of Nazareth in Galilee to Judea, to the city of David called Bethlehem, because he was descended from the house and family of David. He went to be registered with Mary, to whom he was engaged and who was expecting a child.

Where I used to live in Yorkshire was widely known as Herriot Country because of its association with James Herriot of the vet stories fame. People come from far and wide to see it. Bethlehem was often known as 'the house of David' because of its connection to Israel's most famous king. Now its fame rests on being the birthplace of Jesus too.

Local pride is important, yet this must have been the last thing on Joseph's mind as he received the command to go to his hometown. The decree came at an inconvenient time because of Mary's pregnancy. Long journeys were hazardous at the best of times, and now Joseph had this added anxiety to deal with. Joseph was being summoned home to his roots through events beyond his control, yet they would lead to the fulfilment of an ancient prophecy recorded in Micah.

We hear this prophecy read at Christmas, and Bethlehem takes centre stage. But what was it like for Mary and Joseph to set out on the long journey back to family roots? It would demand every ounce of faith on their part to go on believing what they had already understood God to have said to each of them. Perhaps they discussed the visit of the angel to Mary and Joseph's dream as they travelled. Maybe it was only later that they realised God really was in control.

What helps us to keep going when we feel out of control of events? We may not have received a dream, but when our roots are encouraged to grow in our trust in the Lord Jesus, we can remain steady and upright in the middle of the storm.

Where are your roots?

LIZ HOARE

Bethlehem: where fear turns to joy

The angel said to [the shepherds], 'Do not be afraid; for see – I am bringing you good news of great joy for all the people: to you is born this day in the city of David a Saviour, who is the Messiah, the Lord. This will be a sign for you: you will find a child wrapped in bands of cloth and lying in a manger.' And suddenly there was with the angel a multitude of the heavenly host, praising God and saying, 'Glory to God in the highest heaven, and on earth peace among those whom he favours!'

What is it like to have an experience that leaves you eaten up by fear so strong that you are paralysed by it, only for that crippling feeling to turn into overwhelming joy? The angel told the shepherds not to be afraid, yet fear is a fundamental human experience that cripples and destroys human lives everywhere, and for many there is no way out. In the meeting of the shepherds with the angelic host, fear was turned to joy, but only as they got up and left their sheep to go and find out if the angel's message was true. As they went in obedience to investigate, they saw wonders they would never forget and their whole perspective was changed.

Could such a change occur for someone gripped by fear today? Many of our fears boil down to anxiety about fitting in, being accepted by the group, being considered okay. The shepherds might have expected rejection in Bethlehem, being of a lowly and despised profession on the edge of society. Instead, in the presence of this little family they found a welcome and became honoured guests. Jesus came to seek and to save the lost – people like the shepherds, poor, lowly and rejected by society.

For anyone eaten up by fear of any kind today, there is good news. We too can find the same peace and joy promised at the Saviour's birth. As yet a little baby, Jesus was already changing lives. No wonder that when he began his adult ministry, the common people heard him gladly.

Pray that peace and joy will replace fear in your own life
and those closest to you.

LIZ HOARE

Is there anything good in Nazareth?

Philip found Nathanael and said to him, 'We have found him about whom Moses in the law and also the prophets wrote, Jesus son of Joseph from Nazareth.' Nathanael said to him, 'Can anything good come out of Nazareth?' Philip said to him, 'Come and see.' When Jesus saw Nathanael coming towards him, he said of him, 'Here truly is an Israelite in whom there is no deceit!'

If you go to Nazareth today, you might be tempted to wonder if anything has changed since Nathanael dismissed it as a place of no account. It is an Arab town in the hill country, 70 miles north of Jerusalem, poor and unprepossessing.

And yet there is so much more. Pilgrims who are disappointed at what they find in this noisy, dusty town continue to visit, because it was the place where Jesus grew up and spent the first 30 years of his life. Those years are hidden to us and clearly they were also hidden to his contemporaries. Nazareth had nothing about it to suggest that something or someone significant would emerge from its inhabitants. Nathanael, a pious Jew who seems to have lived in expectancy of God's promised deliverer, was, like everyone else, unimpressed with Nazareth. His encounter with the carpenter from its community changed all that, for the stranger seemed to see right into him and to know him.

Nathanael was undone by his meeting with Jesus, and then we hear nothing more about him. Did John name him because he was known to the early church as a believer? He passes in and out of the story, a tiny cameo, yet of infinite significance to the God who sees. Known or unknown, the world's opinion matters little in the light of being known by God. We see a shabby town; God sees every heart that makes up the habitations of this world and loves what he sees. In Nazareth, Jesus had learned to observe with his heavenly Father's eyes and to understand the human heart in all its complexity.

'God chose what is low and despised in the world, even things that are not'
(1 Corinthians 1:28).

LIZ HOARE

A righteous man in Nazareth

When his mother Mary had been engaged to Joseph, but before they lived together, she was found to be with child from the Holy Spirit. Her husband Joseph, being a righteous man and unwilling to expose her to public disgrace, planned to dismiss her quietly. But just when he had resolved to do this, an angel of the Lord appeared to him in a dream and said, 'Joseph, son of David, do not be afraid to take Mary as your wife, for the child conceived in her is from the Holy Spirit.'

There are many myths surrounding Joseph, partly because he fades out of the gospel narrative so quickly. He is, for example, assumed to be old and weak, as he makes no impression on events after the birth. Joseph may have been old, but he was not weak.

In our passage today the important word is 'righteous' (some translations use 'just'), which usually refers to someone who obeys the law and applies rules fairly to everyone. Here it is used to describe Joseph, a man who desired to do the right thing. The law of Moses required a betrothed virgin who became pregnant to be stoned, yet Joseph, being righteous, decided to ignore the law and divorce Mary quietly so as not to expose her publicly.

This could sound strange if we imagine righteousness to be about keeping the rules. What would such righteousness look like today? It could easily describe someone who never broke the law, but also never went out of their way to show mercy to another person in trouble. Joseph went beyond the ethical expectations of the law in obedience to a higher definition of what was just. The prophet Isaiah insisted that justice included compassion for the weak and downtrodden (Isaiah 1:17), and Joseph lived this out faithfully. It was the action of a courageous and compassionate man, a righteous man.

Notice that he took this course of action before, not after, the angel visited him in his dream. How should we translate this kind of righteousness into a way of life for all today? It must begin with us.

Lord, show us how to live according to your ways in our world today. Amen

LIZ HOARE

Growing up in Nazareth

Then [Jesus] went down with [his parents] and came to Nazareth, and was obedient to them. His mother treasured all these things in her heart. And Jesus increased in wisdom and in years, and in divine and human favour.

To be blessed with divine and human favour is to be blessed indeed. The religious leaders in Jerusalem recognised there was something special about Jesus when he was just twelve, yet here he is obediently going home with his parents to an obscure town. This passage completes what we know of Jesus' life before his public ministry. After the birth stories, we have only this glimpse of his childhood and then silence until his baptism.

For 30 years, Jesus lived a life of obscurity doing… what exactly? What more could his parents, simple people, have to teach him? How did he fill his days? Whatever it was that occupied his time and energy, we may be sure he found God in it all, and all of it contributed to his growth in wisdom and in divine and human favour. We tend to assume that Jesus knew everything, because he was God, but he chose to limit himself and become the same as all humans, growing from childhood to maturity.

This gives us a great insight into the merciful humility of God. Like the rest of Nazareth's inhabitants, the home, his neighbours, his daily labours, the people down the street and the local synagogue had a part to play in how Jesus grew. And all without fame, drama or constant stimulation. This is a huge encouragement to the vast majority of us who live ordinary lives, bringing up children, commuting to work, looking after an elderly relative, tending a garden or cleaning a public place. Learning to discover God in the hidden places of the world, like Nazareth, leads to wisdom and maturity that is more precious than gold itself. Insignificant Jesus' life may have been at this stage, but it was the crucible in which he grew up into the adult who was beloved and delighted in by God.

Look back over the past 24 hours, giving thanks for where you become aware of God's presence in what has occurred, and ask for wisdom for tomorrow.

LIZ HOARE

A surprising visitor to Nazareth

In the sixth month the angel Gabriel was sent by God to a town in Galilee called Nazareth, to a virgin engaged to a man whose name was Joseph, of the house of David. The virgin's name was Mary. And he came to her and said, 'Greetings, favoured one! The Lord is with you.' But she was much perplexed by his words and pondered what sort of greeting this might be. The angel said to her, 'Do not be afraid, Mary, for you have found favour with God.'

Nazareth is not mentioned in the Old Testament, but as the town where Jesus grew up and where Mary was visited by the angel Gabriel, its importance to the Christian story is firmly established. It produced Joseph, a man who was just and compassionate. Luke here introduces us to Mary, a young girl, growing up in her home, unaware of what was going to be asked of her.

Our impressions of Mary are formed by the church tradition we belong to and perhaps by how she is depicted in film and other artworks. But what kind of a woman was she? She is often portrayed as beautiful and saintly, on a pedestal (sometimes literally), beyond our reach. While the Catholic tradition venerates her and, often in reaction to that, Protestants may ignore her, Luke shows us a real human being invited to play a critical role in God's plan of salvation.

It is easy to overlook the magnitude of the angel's message or to hurry on past Mary's perplexity to her agreement to submit to God's will. She was given an invitation, however, not an order, and her fear at the angel's greeting was real and acknowledged. Calling her by name, Gabriel told her not to be afraid. Not only was God with her, but he also looked at her with favour. Why did God choose her? We do not know, but one thing is clear: God risked entrusting the Saviour of all humanity to this young woman. While we do not know how Mary brought Jesus up, she must have influenced his attitude towards people in general and women in particular at their home in Nazareth.

Reflect on God's risky strategy of entrusting himself to men and women and his promise to be with us.

LIZ HOARE

Launching a mission in Nazareth

When [Jesus] came to Nazareth, where he had been brought up, he went to the synagogue on the sabbath day, as was his custom. He stood up to read, and the scroll of the prophet Isaiah was given to him. He unrolled the scroll and found the place where it was written: 'The Spirit of the Lord is upon me, because he has anointed me to bring good news to the poor. He has sent me to proclaim release to the captives and recovery of sight to the blind, to let the oppressed go free, to proclaim the year of the Lord's favour'… Then he began to say to them, 'Today this scripture has been fulfilled in your hearing.'

When we meet someone who inspires us with their outlook on life or vision for the world, we love to discover where it all began. What influenced them when they were growing up? Where did their inspiration come from?

Jesus grew up in Nazareth, and it was the place he chose to launch his ministry. Is it surprising that he chose his hometown, 'where he had been brought up', to explain that here and now Isaiah's prophecy was being fulfilled in the hearing of those present? Surely he realised that no one would take any notice of Joseph's son, for they all knew him. He was a familiar figure in the synagogue. Jesus knew the saying that a prophet was unwelcome in his hometown, but he chose to begin with those nearest to him. They needed to hear the good news too.

When I visited the synagogue in Nazareth recently, I also went into the nearby Anglican church where a small, mostly elderly congregation seeks to live out the good news of Jesus in their words and their actions. Nazareth was first to hear the good news of spiritual freedom, healing and blessing and the first to show hostility to one of its own. Yet perhaps there was someone who listened and at some point became a follower. Somehow, the year of the Lord's favour did take root here and elsewhere in Jesus' homeland and has not been extinguished. It is an encouragement to keep on spreading the good news in our hometowns.

Pray for small and struggling but still faithful Christian churches in the Holy Land today.

LIZ HOARE

The teacher from Nazareth

Pilate also had an inscription written and put on the cross. It read, 'Jesus of Nazareth, the King of the Jews.' Many of the Jews read this inscription, because the place where Jesus was crucified was near the city; and it was written in Hebrew, in Latin, and in Greek. Then the chief priests of the Jews said to Pilate, 'Do not write, "The King of the Jews", but, "This man said, I am King of the Jews."' Pilate answered, 'What I have written I have written.'

The entire story of Jesus' earthly life and ministry can be bookended with reference to Nazareth, beginning with the proclamation in the synagogue and ending with his final breath on the cross. Jesus' hometown formed part of the story that continues to be told.

The Jewish leaders did not object to Jesus being described as 'of Nazareth' but to his being given the title 'the King of the Jews'. No one disputed the human story; Jesus was Joseph's son from an obscure northern town. But the religious leaders realised the seriousness of saying anything more. He may have healed the sick, given sight to the blind, even raised the dead, but to agree that he was God's beloved Son would demand so much more.

Many people today acknowledge that Jesus existed, that he was a good man, even a great teacher, but they refuse to go the next step and declare him to be Lord and Saviour of the world. Many of us believe that this means he must be Lord of our lives, too, and that means we will need to make changes in how we live. The teacher from Nazareth, as Pilate's inscription acknowledged, is so much more than just a man.

What about us? Are we content to go along with the creeds in our heads that proclaim Jesus' divinity without letting it touch us in our hearts and change our values and actions? What difference does it make in daily decisions for you and me to say, 'This is the king,' rather than, 'He said, I am the king'?

Pray for someone you know who is struggling with believing that Jesus is who he says he is.

LIZ HOARE

In the name of Jesus of Nazareth

Peter said, 'I have no silver or gold, but what I have I give you; in the name of Jesus Christ of Nazareth, stand up and walk.' And he took him by the right hand and raised him up; and immediately his feet and ankles were made strong. Jumping up, he stood and began to walk, and he entered the temple with them, walking and leaping and praising God.

We have left the gospels behind, but Nazareth continues to feature in the early days of the church. Despite the resurrection and the coming of the Holy Spirit in power upon the first believers, they still referred to him as Jesus of Nazareth. He would forever be the man from Galilee who changed lives.

Peter and John, two of Jesus' closest disciples, were doing what they saw Jesus doing during his earthly ministry. They preached the good news and they healed the sick, just as Jesus taught them to do. For three years they had accompanied Jesus in and around Galilee, watching him, listening to him and then being sent out to do the same themselves. The difference now was the assurance brought by the resurrection and the seal of the Holy Spirit in their lives. Confident in the power of the name of Jesus of Nazareth, they proclaimed to their contemporaries the good news that the promises of God were 'for you, for your children, and for all who are far away, everyone whom the Lord our God calls to him' (Acts 2:39), including the lame beggar at the gate of the temple in our passage.

The power of the name of Jesus of Nazareth has never been extinguished. We too may find courage in the name. We too may find our struggles strangely filled with joy, our lives turned around, our hope restored. In a world obsessed with silver and gold, fame and fortune, this is a completely upside-down way of living. But people still join in and follow the man from Nazareth. The challenge is to us and our children too.

What will 'walking and leaping and praising God' look like for you this coming week?

LIZ HOARE

1 and 2 Peter

The letters of Peter claim a single author and share many common themes. They are, however, separated in time and deal with contexts that appear to have developed considerably.

Writing to dispersed Christian communities, Peter in his first letter invites a strong and steady faith in God in the face of increasing hostility. The experience of suffering and how this stands alongside the call to be true to God is a dominant theme. This means that Peter is deeply concerned with the quality and solidity of the faith of the Christian communities. He sets their faith in the context of all eternity and aims to show that as Christ suffered, and was destined to, they must also suffer with him if they will share in his glory. This faith is not an inward, private matter; it impacts our relationships within the church, our relationships with those closest to us, how we give account of the hope we have and how we relate to a world that is challenging and at times deeply hostile to the gospel. Leaders are addressed too, because Christ's care and suffering also provide them with a pattern for living and ministry.

Above all of this, 1 Peter sets the eternal purposes of God, promised in the Old Testament and now revealed in Jesus, as the basis of his gospel. The death and resurrection of Jesus not only offer a pattern for living but also fundamentally control the very destiny of the world and all Christian people. We are to stand in the grace given to us, rejoicing in the goal of our faith with inexpressible joy.

2 Peter builds on these themes. The author's conviction is that the world is even more hostile to the gospel than in former years and that challenges abound. Christians are called to grow in godliness and to avoid the excesses of the world, which might lure some into abandoning their faith. We are to wait for the promised coming of Christ, which is sure and certain even if God's timing is not ours to know. But a steady and sure commitment to Christ, to grow in grace, shows we belong to him and will be his for all eternity.

ANDY JOHN

A living faith

Praise be to the God and Father of our Lord Jesus Christ! In his great mercy he has given us new birth into a living hope through the resurrection of Jesus Christ from the dead, and into an inheritance that can never perish, spoil or fade. This inheritance is kept in heaven for you, who through faith are shielded by God's power until the coming of the salvation that is ready to be revealed in the last time. In all this you greatly rejoice, though now for a little while you may have had to suffer grief in all kinds of trials. These have come so that the proven genuineness of your faith – of greater worth than gold, which perishes even though refined by fire – may result in praise, glory and honour when Jesus Christ is revealed.

In this first passage Peter explores the quality of Christian faith. First, it is 'living'. Faith like this is more than any simple recital of a creed. It is living, because it is nourished and active. Stagnant faith can never support a living faith any more than a stagnant pond any real life. When we nourish our faith, the sustaining work of his Spirit becomes real.

Second, it is shielding. I have been grateful when walking in the hills to find shelters from squally weather! Those places keep us dry and safe. Faith in Christ is like this because, although the shelters do not stop the rains and winds, they do offer protection. This does not mean we do not encounter difficulties but that we are not overcome by them. God's care, however fierce the storm, is steady and real.

Last, this faith is refined and proved genuine. When we experience difficulties, perhaps illness or uncertainty, it can seem as though we are powerless and all is meaningless. But I have learned the most sustaining things about myself and the Lord at these times. These have become a part of my walk into the future, informing my decisions and sustaining me.

Lord, faith in you is a priceless treasure. Help us to attend to everyday life in a way which nourishes faith in you. Amen

ANDY JOHN

Faith choices

As obedient children, do not conform to the evil desires you had when you lived in ignorance. But just as he who called you is holy, so be holy in all you do; for it is written: 'Be holy, because I am holy.' Since you call on a Father who judges each person's work impartially, live out your time as foreigners here in reverent fear... He was chosen before the creation of the world, but was revealed in these last times for your sake. Through him you believe in God... and so your faith and hope are in God. Now that you have purified yourselves by obeying the truth so that you have sincere love for each other, love one another deeply, from the heart.

Faith that is consciously exercised has consequences. Today Peter explains how faith challenges worthless choices and opens up new life. He also shows that a new perspective is required – faith is not some appendage, but it controls every part of us.

This perspective is vital. Peter urges a different approach to life, because his readers now know the truth of the gospel. In order to both honour God and grow in their faith, they need to practise the divine 'No' as well as the divine 'Yes'.

This is challenging for us because our instincts often move in the other direction. We need the bigger picture to remind us of the price of our salvation, but we also need the active grace of God that is ours in Christ each day.

Faith also invites a positive outlook on life. We are not merely to cease from harmful choices but to practise healthy ones. We are to love one another deeply from the heart. In a world in which love is often either misunderstood or absent, this is radical. When Christians love like this, we show the transforming love of Christ and how each of us can be restored to a way of living that is less self-serving and more liberating.

Lord Jesus, stand at the very heart of my life and transform my faith
so that others might be deeply blessed. Amen

ANDY JOHN

Out of darkness

Now to you who believe, this stone is precious. But to those who do not believe, 'The stone the builders rejected has become the cornerstone,' and, 'A stone that causes people to stumble and a rock that makes them fall.' They stumble because they disobey the message... But you are a chosen people, a royal priesthood, a holy nation, God's special possession, that you may declare the praises of him who called you out of darkness into his wonderful light. Once you were not a people, but now you are the people of God; once you had not received mercy, but now you have received mercy.

In today's passage, Peter links the identity of the new church with the Jerusalem temple, the holy nation and the worship offered by priests.

Like the temple, the church is a place in which God's presence is known; here God is worshipped and adored. As I write this, the fire that engulfed Notre Dame in Paris has just been extinguished. You may recall footage of the huge spire collapsing as the fire took hold. But Peter does not see the church as a building that can be destroyed by fire. The stones of this church, he says, are 'living', and, though they are dispersed across the world, they are one in Christ, forming a spiritual house.

Peter also sees the church as a redefined Israel. Just as the covenant and the law set apart the holy nation, Israel, so in Christ those promises come to all who belong to him. We are heirs of those treasures given to Abraham and Moses.

The third grace given to us is the priestly practices. But the sacrifices offered are not to bring about a restored relationship with God – that is ours through the work of the cross. It is the sacrifice of lives given in loving service to God and the world.

These three graces, then – God's presence, promises and practices – are essential to the nature of the church. And Christ at the centre is constantly at work in us so these things grow and reveal God to a world in need of redeeming love.

Lord, you have given us so much. May your grace grow in me that I might declare your praises to a world yet to know the Saviour's love. Amen

ANDY JOHN

43

Authorities and masters

Live as free people, but do not use your freedom as a cover-up for evil; live as God's slaves. Show proper respect to everyone, love the family of believers, fear God, honour the emperor. Slaves, in reverent fear of God submit yourselves to your masters, not only to those who are good and considerate, but also to those who are harsh. For it is commendable if someone bears up under the pain of unjust suffering because they are conscious of God. But how is it to your credit if you receive a beating for doing wrong and endure it? But if you suffer for doing good and you endure it, this is commendable before God.

We have seen that Peter is focused on how his fellow Christians suffer for the sake of Christ. We need this perspective to understand our reading today. A simplistic reading would lead us to conclude that we should be overly passive towards those in authority and ambivalent about slavery.

Peter provides two arenas in which Christians should witness. First, in relation to the state, he calls for obedience to authority in order to silence foolish and destructive talk. We can imagine that Christians who profess faith in Jesus but live at odds with this faith would be a scandal. In other words, Peter is advocating the virtue of endurance and how this Christlikeness compels a response (for good or ill).

Second, Peter engages with slaves, who likewise could show they belonged to Christ by enduring hardship. His appeal is to the power of Christian testimony, and we too will have heard extraordinary stories of Christians who overcame or forgave when their suffering or circumstances invited a different response.

This attitude does not mean holding an uncritical acceptance of the status quo, nor does it mean that Christians today should tolerate slavery in any shape or form. There must always be a prophetic counterculture that is prepared to challenge what is wrong and unjust. But in addition to this, we are reminded of the need to witness to the salvation found in Jesus, whatever the consequences of our faith.

Suffering Lord, may our story of trusting you in good and hard times reach those who do not know you and invite them home. Amen

ANDY JOHN

Husbands and wives

Wives, in the same way submit yourselves to your own husbands so that, if any of them do not believe the word, they may be won over without words by the behaviour of their wives, when they see the purity and reverence of your lives. Your beauty should not come from outward adornment, such as elaborate hairstyles and the wearing of gold jewellery or fine clothes. Rather, it should be that of your inner self, the unfading beauty of a gentle and quiet spirit, which is of great worth in God's sight. For this is the way the holy women of the past who put their hope in God used to adorn themselves. They submitted themselves to their own husbands.

The cultural gap between our world today and the one in which Peter wrote is laid bare in this reading. Some of us might read this and simply embrace the instruction without further thought; others might entirely dismiss it as another example of patriarchy which is beyond rescue. I want to offer you a different reading in order to explore some of the profound beauty and wisdom remaining in this passage.

Peter is deeply committed to mutuality and how harmony witnesses to the Lord Jesus. The instructions he provides are underpinned by a commitment to a shared relationship. Marriage will not happen by accident but through serious investment on the part of both parties. He also sees that there are things that can inhibit strong relationships, such as materialism. There is therefore a realism in his counsel to be invested positively in one's partner as well as to recognise what can damage and mar that relationship.

Our relationships can witness to Christ, as we saw in yesterday's reading. What fosters healthy relationships are the deeper, better things crafted over time, such as love, respect and support. It is not that jewellery or clothes are themselves wrong but that better realities can be hidden by a shallowness made up of any misplaced priorities.

Lord, give me what I need to make good relationships flourish around me and to be a source of grace and goodness in Jesus' name. Amen

ANDY JOHN

Descending to save

For Christ also suffered once for sins, the righteous for the unrighteous, to bring you to God. He was put to death in the body but made alive in the Spirit. After being made alive, he went and made proclamation to the imprisoned spirits – to those who were disobedient long ago when God waited patiently in the days of Noah while the ark was being built. In it only a few people, eight in all, were saved through water, and this water symbolises baptism that now saves you also – not the removal of dirt from the body but the pledge of a clear conscience towards God. It saves you by the resurrection of Jesus Christ, who has gone into heaven and is at God's right hand – with angels, authorities and powers in submission to him.

We have seen that Peter encourages his readers to stand firm in the face of suffering. He has already presented Christ as being an example for us when we are under pressure and a guarantee of a future relationship with him. Today's reading is one of the more unusual passages and lies behind the statement in the Apostles' Creed that Jesus Christ 'descended to the dead'. But what does it mean?

The descent of Christ has been variously understood. For some, it is about the way those lost prior to Christ's resurrection would hear the gospel and be saved. In this way it allows the saving grace of Christ to work backwards. Others have emphasised that it is not a preaching of invitation but a declaration of triumph. Christ descends so that even the abode of the dead would know he has been victorious.

We must remember that Peter's focus is on righteous suffering. The emphasis is not so much on what he achieves by his descent but that, because he descends, he is truly the Saviour. It is obedience that brings Christ to triumph and victory in heaven with powers and authorities in submission to him.

Lord Jesus Christ, you descended to the dead and preached to those imprisoned. We too have heard your voice and seen your glory, suffering Lord. May we now live for you, our holy and righteous king. Amen

ANDY JOHN

Facing the future with God

Therefore, since Christ suffered in his body, arm yourselves also with the same attitude, because whoever suffers in the body has finished with sin. As a result, they do not live the rest of their earthly lives for evil human desires, but rather for the will of God… The end of all things is near. Therefore be alert and of sober mind so that you may pray. Above all, love each other deeply, because love covers over a multitude of sins. Offer hospitality to one another without grumbling. Each of you should use whatever gift you have received to serve others, as faithful stewards of God's grace in its various forms. If anyone speaks, they should do so as one who speaks the very words of God. If anyone serves, they should do so with the strength God provides, so that in all things God may be praised through Jesus Christ.

In our passage today, Peter explores two themes: how the radical message of the gospel compels a break with the past, and how the end of all things and the return of Christ invite a new behaviour.

We cannot continue in a life of self-centredness now that we have tasted the goodness of God. This message is consistent with the apostles' teaching. Paul asked the Roman Christians whether we could 'go on sinning, so that grace may increase', then answered, 'By no means! We are those who have died to sin; how can we live in it any longer?' (Romans 6:1–2).

But new life is not only breaking from a sinful past; it is also living a new Christlikeness. We are to reflect him as we wait for his coming – in love and hospitality, in exercising our gifts to serve and in speaking as though with the very words of Christ. These things bring praise to God and properly reflect our identity as followers of Christ. Although we live with daily failings, the trajectory is heaven bound and therefore we live in constant readiness here and now.

Lord, you have called us from darkness and fitted us for heaven.
Give us grace to live like this each day. Amen

ANDY JOHN

Suffering like Christ

Dear friends, do not be surprised at the fiery ordeal that has come on you to test you, as though something strange were happening to you. But rejoice inasmuch as you participate in the sufferings of Christ, so that you may be overjoyed when his glory is revealed. If you are insulted because of the name of Christ, you are blessed, for the Spirit of glory and of God rests on you. If you suffer, it should not be as a murderer or thief or any other kind of criminal, or even as a meddler. However, if you suffer as a Christian, do not be ashamed, but praise God that you bear that name.

Peter returns to his central theme, but with three exhortations, which are transformational. We have seen that he expects the church to suffer and that this is a mark of authenticity.

Peter suggests two responses to suffering that should be avoided. First, we should not be surprised. If the church wishes to be like its master, it will suffer. This is because Christian faith confronts godlessness and is likely to face opposition. More profoundly, without suffering there can be no church. If Christ's life was marked by suffering, can that of his body (that is, his church) be any different?

Second, we ought not to be ashamed. Suffering is easily confused with failure, and some might have regarded the suffering of Christians as evidence that their faith was foolish. Peter exhorts his readers not to conspire with this view. To suffer with Christ is blessed.

To these two exhortations, Peter adds something extraordinary: we should rejoice in suffering with Christ. He does not say we rejoice because we suffer; rather, the focus is on the one for whose sake we suffer. And this is because suffering makes possible a deeper relationship with God. Countless Christians have found here a source of consolation. To suffer, as did Christ, does not lessen the intensity of what we experience but offers the potential for it to be received differently. It is this which makes rejoicing possible.

Lord Christ, to live with you may I be strengthened to suffer with you and rejoice in seeing your glory. Amen

ANDY JOHN

Lessons for all

To the elders among you, I appeal as a fellow elder and a witness of Christ's sufferings who also will share in the glory to be revealed: be shepherds of God's flock that is under your care, watching over them – not because you must, but because you are willing, as God wants you to be; not pursuing dishonest gain, but eager to serve; not lording it over those entrusted to you, but being examples to the flock. And when the Chief Shepherd appears, you will receive the crown of glory that will never fade away. In the same way, you who are younger, submit yourselves to your elders. All of you, clothe yourselves with humility towards one another, because, 'God opposes the proud but shows favour to the humble.' Humble yourselves, therefore, under God's mighty hand, that he may lift you up in due time. Cast all your anxiety on him because he cares for you.

Peter addresses different groups in his letter today: leaders, younger Christians and believers generally. He continues to refer to the sufferings of Christ as the pattern for Christian living, but introduces the image of a shepherd. This must relate to what he has previously written. What is the connection?

A shepherd is responsible for the safety of the flock. The job of shepherding requires certain skills in order to protect and care for each sheep. The implication is that the shepherd of the Christian flock must also be skilled, but this is about the personal disciplines of faithfulness to Christ. For instance, leaders are not to be greedy but eager to serve. Oversight cannot happen unless leaders are practising these habits personally.

If they are required in leaders, such virtues are also commended to others: the younger are to be respectful, and all are to practise humility. Self-control is vital, because our inner life is the arena in which character is formed and by God's grace, we are shaped into the image of Christ. It is impossible for us to live faithfully if there is disorder in our lives.

Lord, in the realities of life, let suffering not be wasted in me but mould, shape and form in me the character I need to please you in life and in ministry. Amen

ANDY JOHN

Joined to God

For this very reason, make every effort to add to your faith goodness; and to goodness, knowledge; and to knowledge, self-control; and to self-control, perseverance; and to perseverance, godliness; and to godliness, mutual affection; and to mutual affection, love. For if you possess these qualities in increasing measure, they will keep you from being ineffective and unproductive in your knowledge of our Lord Jesus Christ. But whoever does not have them is short-sighted and blind, forgetting that they have been cleansed from their past sins. Therefore, my brothers and sisters, make every effort to confirm your calling and election. For if you do these things, you will never stumble, and you will receive a rich welcome into the eternal kingdom of our Lord and Saviour Jesus Christ.

Today we move on to the second letter in the name of the apostle. Some have wondered whether this is the same author as that of the first letter. Others have pointed out that writing styles develop and that any differences are easily accounted for by the fact that this is an older apostle writing.

The themes of 2 Peter are similar to its predecessor, but it offers new insights and challenges too. For example, in today's passage Peter develops something new concerning our identity as Christians. We are to make our election sure and to do this by adding to Spirit-inspired virtues that make us effective and productive. In other words, we know we belong to Christ because the gospel produces a life that reflects the character of the Lord Jesus. Paul listed love, joy and peace among other things as the fruit of God's Spirit in his letter to the Galatians (5:22), and Jesus preached about fruitfulness as the sign of authentic grace (Matthew 7:15–20).

Fruit exists, of course, not simply as proof of a tree's health but for the benefit of others. Faith that is laden with fruit will be a source of blessing: the naked will be clothed, the hungry fed and the fallen lifted up.

Lord Jesus Christ, may good fruit grow in me, strengthen my faith and become a source of blessing to others. Amen

ANDY JOHN

Solid ground

So I will always remind you of these things, even though you know them and are firmly established in the truth you now have. I think it is right to refresh your memory as long as I live in the tent of this body, because I know that I will soon put it aside, as our Lord Jesus Christ has made clear to me. And I will make every effort to see that after my departure you will always be able to remember these things. For we did not follow cleverly devised stories when we told you about the coming of our Lord Jesus Christ in power, but we were eyewitnesses of his majesty… We ourselves heard this voice that came from heaven when we were with him on the sacred mountain. We also have the prophetic message as something completely reliable.

Peter rehearses a familiar story to remind his readers of the basis of their faith. The gospel, promised long ago, has its origins in the Old Testament. Why does Peter remind them of something so familiar?

First, because he wishes to leave a good legacy. Many of us will recall how wise and godly Christians made an impact on us, and how they helped us meet the future well. Is there any better legacy than a living faith passed down to others?

Second, to underscore the enduring faithfulness of God, who spoke through the prophets. The gospel is true from all ages and does not mark some strange shift by God, but is evidence of God's eternal providence.

Third, the very act of reminding is a powerful way of keeping alive what is bequeathed. How often do we sing hymns that remind us of the great gospel truths? They make more immediate the treasures of faith and strengthen us. So when Peter recalls the transfiguration described in the gospels (Matthew 17:5), it is not to rehearse a creed but to make Christ real and certain in the lives of his readers.

Lord, you confirm our faith in many ways. May our memory of you stir new and living faith in us today. Amen

ANDY JOHN

Mists and storms

But there were also false prophets among the people, just as there will be false teachers among you. They will secretly introduce destructive heresies, even denying the sovereign Lord who bought them – bringing swift destruction on themselves. Many will follow their depraved conduct and will bring the way of truth into disrepute. In their greed these teachers will exploit you with fabricated stories. Their condemnation has long been hanging over them, and their destruction has not been sleeping.

Peter unleashes explosive preaching against all who undermine the gospel. His focus is on those who have now abandoned the faith and returned to the life they once lived, denying Christ – to their destruction.

Why is Peter forthright in his condemnation of this? The key to understanding the force of his words lies in the consequences of heresy. He begins by noting how false prophets have appeared, leading astray those who follow them. That way – a heady mix of narcissism, greed and ignorance – brings misery and disaster, as described in the rest of the chapter.

The relationship between faith and behaviour is important. But we need to be clear about a number of things here. First, we are not saved by possessing an orthodox faith, but rather by Christ's free and unmerited love and favour towards us. The gospel is about what Christ has achieved, which we could not. Peter is not therefore commending an orthodoxy that gets us to heaven. Second, his concern is that an abandoned faith leads to an abandoned lifestyle with all restraint removed.

And this shows that being grounded in the gospel secures that closer walk with God needed by everyone. A framework of solid faith is like the armour of God promised in Ephesians: 'Therefore put on the full armour of God, so that when the day of evil comes, you may be able to stand your ground' (6:13). Preaching like this in the scriptures is not here to cajole but as a warning and boundary so that we can be secure in following what Christ has given us.

---

*Lord, keep before us the boundaries of faith that help us
remain close to you and your ways. Amen*

ANDY JOHN

New heaven, new earth

They will say, 'Where is this "coming" he promised? Ever since our ancestors died, everything goes on as it has since the beginning of creation.' But they deliberately forget that long ago by God's word the heavens came into being and the earth was formed out of water and by water… But do not forget this one thing, dear friends: with the Lord a day is like a thousand years, and a thousand years are like a day. The Lord is not slow in keeping his promise, as some understand slowness. Instead he is patient with you, not wanting anyone to perish, but everyone to come to repentance… Since everything will be destroyed in this way, what kind of people ought you to be? You ought to live holy and godly lives… But in keeping with his promise we are looking forward to a new heaven and a new earth, where righteousness dwells.

In today's passage, Peter deals with a threat that appears to have emerged. The return of Christ had not materialised, and some were wondering if they (or worse, Christ) were mistaken. If mistaken on this, was the gospel itself reliable and trustworthy?

Peter's response is threefold. He reminds his readers that God is Lord over all creation. This is vital today, as we face earnest questions about our future as human beings. Faith ought not to make us complacent; we are responsible to God for the proper care and stewardship of all creation.

Then, Peter asserts that God does not operate to our timescale. Our finite perspective could lead to the conclusion that Christ will not return. But this would be a mistake. The timing of such an end is God's to make and the manner too.

Finally, Peter points out that the end of former things will lead to a new heaven and earth. The scale and magnitude of this is beyond our comprehension, perhaps, but its effect is more immediate – we are to live godly and holy lives, fit for the new creation, where Christ is Lord of all.

Lord, give me that preparedness that sees the distant scene
and that lives in the day-to-day for your glory. Amen.

ANDY JOHN

Grow in grace

Bear in mind that our Lord's patience means salvation… Therefore, dear friends, since you have been forewarned, be on your guard so that you may not be carried away by the error of the lawless and fall from your secure position. But grow in the grace and knowledge of our Lord and Saviour Jesus Christ. To him be glory both now and forever! Amen

Peter draws his letter to a close by urging patience in the light of the sure coming of Christ. The delay in Christ's return is due to forbearance and ought not to be regarded as uncertain. He also commends faithfulness to the teaching they have received, including that of Paul, which some were distorting. Finally, he encourages them to grow in grace and the knowledge of God and Christ.

These last words are a fitting end and bear further thought. How do we grow in grace and knowledge? Much of Peter's attention has been with the external pressures on the church – persecution and heresy – and the effects they have on faith and discipleship. These provide part of the answer, in as much as pressure has always produced either new strength or rupture. The challenge for us is to allow hardship to generate godliness and depth rather than a diminished faith. This mindset allows us to see trouble positively rather than as a waste.

But implicit in all Peter has said are things that sustain our relationship with Christ, like joy, hunger for his presence, love, goodness and a grounding in the gospel. The practice of holy habits provides the stepping stones we need to continue our walk with God. For those early Christians, it would be in these disciplines that their life in Christ would either grow or stagnate. Our situation is quite different from theirs, but the challenge is much the same. Whatever hardships we face, there is the invitation to choose Christ, to remain close and to never abandon faith. May we grow in the grace and knowledge of our Lord and Saviour Jesus Christ. Amen

---

Lord, you have called us out of darkness to declare your praises.
May your presence be always with us and your glory always seen in us
for your endless praise. Amen

ANDY JOHN

A pilgrim heart

As part of my work, I lecture and lead workshops on pilgrimage. I cover all aspects of pilgrimage spirituality – its history, its practice and its place in the life of the church today. Often I begin by showing a picture of me on pilgrimage, which I describe as 'me at my best' – being most fully the person God has called me to be. But this concept has its problems, because I cannot spend all my time making pilgrimages – I have a church, a family, a home, friends and neighbours, commitments and obligations. After much prayer and reflection, I realised that I needed to take the most significant aspects of pilgrimage, its effects and its blessings, and incorporate them into my everyday life. Instead of simply referring to life as a journey, I would endeavour to practise those skills that served me well on pilgrimage and use them as best I could in my home surroundings.

One of the gifts of pilgrimage is that it offers the time and the space to reflect, to recharge and to resource ourselves with the wisdom that the road can offer. The following notes are some of the fruit of my times of reflection. I hope they illustrate some of the insights offered by the practice of pilgrimage and show how they can be used to deepen our relationship with God, with our fellow human beings and with ourselves, whether or not we are physically journeying.

For clarity, I use the term pilgrimage to mean a 'spiritual journey to a sacred place'. It can refer to a journey by foot of many days or weeks, or a short walk of a few hours. Journeys using less physical means, such as by car or coach, can have a similar impact, but my personal experience – and these reflections – is drawn from the spirituality of the walked path.

Who would true valour see,
Let him come hither;
One here will constant be,
Come wind, come weather.
There's no discouragement
Shall make him once relent
His first avowed intent
To be a pilgrim.
(John Bunyan, *Pilgrim's Progress*, 1684)

SALLY WELCH

Deciding to go

Then [Pharaoh] said, 'Rise up, go away from my people, both you and the Israelites! Go, worship the Lord, as you said. Take your flocks and your herds, as you said, and be gone. And bring a blessing on me too!' The Egyptians urged the people to hasten their departure from the land, for they said, 'We shall all be dead.' So the people took their dough before it was leavened, with their kneading-bowls wrapped up in their cloaks on their shoulders.

So begins one of the founding events of the Jewish faith – the escape of the children of Israel from slavery in Egypt to the promised land. And what a hasty, hurried event it was! The evening had been spent making what preparations they could for departure, gathering up clothes and possessions into easily portable bundles, making sure small children and animals would be kept safe, saying farewell to familiar surroundings. Then the hours of anxious waiting before the final command initiating that great rush to join the streams of people leaving the land of captivity and heading towards the unknown.

Most pilgrimages do not begin like this. Although I have met pilgrims who were impelled by intense feeling or the powerful impulse of an event to set off with only the most basic of preparations, the majority of pilgrimages are the product of months of planning, training and saving. The project of making a pilgrimage often springs from a small seed of an idea – watching a programme on television, meeting someone who has done a similar journey or reading an inspirational book. Or a pilgrimage can have been a long-term ambition, the pilgrim waiting patiently for the right time and situation before finally committing themselves to the journey.

Similarly with our faith journey – we may be impelled to seek God through a crisis or we may spend much time in debating and pondering on the nature of the unknown. Others may have experienced faith-based living all their lives. All these journeys have their own integrity – all that matters is that we decide to set out.

Lord, hold me by the hand as I step out along your way.

SALLY WELCH

Leaving

'Know that I am with you and will keep you wherever you go, and will bring you back to this land; for I will not leave you until I have done what I have promised you'… Then Jacob made a vow, saying, 'If God will be with me, and will keep me in this way that I go, and will give me bread to eat and clothing to wear, so that I come again to my father's house in peace, then the Lord shall be my God, and this stone, which I have set up for a pillar, shall be God's house; and of all that you give me I will surely give one-tenth to you.'

Jacob has been sent by his father Isaac to visit the home of his maternal grandfather in order to marry. In the night he dreamt of that famous ladder reaching up to heaven, with angels ascending and descending, and he heard God's wonderful promise, 'I am with you.' Now he makes a covenant with God, promising commitment and obedience in return for the gift of God's presence. Such a gift will mean that his journey can be made in confidence, secure in the knowledge that he does not journey alone.

It is a risky business, setting off on a journey, whether the journey is that of deepening our faith, entering into a new relationship or beginning a trek of many days. We may quite rightly be apprehensive about the future, for who knows what will happen to us along the way? What terrors might we meet? What accidents might befall us? But there will be joys as well – times of delight and happiness, when our steps are light and the path is filled with wonder.

If we allow him, God will make Jacob's covenant with each one of us, extending his loving protection over us wherever we go, until he leads us safely home once more. Then we can explore in safety, free to wander along unfamiliar tracks and pathways, sheltered as we are by God's loving hand over us.

'And you will have confidence, because there is hope;
you will be protected and take your rest in safety' (Job 11:18).

SALLY WELCH

How to sing a new song?

O sing to the Lord a new song; sing to the Lord, all the earth. Sing to the Lord, bless his name; tell of his salvation from day to day. Declare his glory among the nations, his marvellous works among all the peoples.

As I have got older, I have become more fond of routine, particularly at the beginning of the day. I like to get up at the same time, whether I am working or on holiday; I like the same food for breakfast and I like to read the newspaper in peace. Going on pilgrimage changes all this – I must get up at a time to suit either my accommodation or my fellow pilgrims; I must eat whatever is provided by the hostel or whatever I can find along the route; I have very little time to read the paper. For the first few days of any pilgrimage, therefore, I feel scratchy and uncomfortable, taken from the familiar framework of my day. Gradually, however, new rhythms emerge that are based around other set features – lacing my boots, filling up my water bottle, pausing to breathe deeply before setting foot outside the door. In time these become such familiar friends that on my return I struggle to adapt to my domestic routine.

Changes to our patterns of life are sometimes welcome – a new arrival into the family, perhaps, or a successful operation bringing relief from pain. Other changes can bring discomfort or suffering – a house or job move, an absence, even a death. We might struggle to adapt, finding it hard to locate God within the new circumstances in which we find ourselves. We might discover that our usual ways of meeting God are inadequate and unsatisfying, experiencing a sense of loss and alienation.

During these times we can find comfort in remembering what God has done for us in the past and how faithfully he has kept his promises to us. Confident of his presence, we can look for ways of singing new songs that will fill us with hope for the journey ahead.

Lord God, you have guarded and guided me in the past;
help me to step forward confidently into the future.

SALLY WELCH

Travelling light

Then Jesus called the twelve together and gave them power and authority over all demons and to cure diseases, and he sent them out to proclaim the kingdom of God and to heal. He said to them, 'Take nothing for your journey, no staff, nor bag, nor bread, nor money – not even an extra tunic.'

Packing for a pilgrimage is a highly skilled activity. On the one hand, it is important to carry all that is necessary to journey successfully and safely – appropriate clothing, food and water, a first aid kit, a phone charger, maps. On the other hand, the heavier the pack, the greater the chances of disaster – tired walkers fall more easily, make navigational mistakes, misjudge dangers. Getting the balance right is vitally important.

In our daily lives, we tread the same tightrope. If we lack the basic necessities, our lives become narrowed, perhaps even shortened. If, however, we surround ourselves with material possessions, we are in danger of being submerged by them, as we turn into guardians of our goods rather than inhabitants of a wider universe. When Jesus sent out his disciples to preach, heal and teach, he sent them with nothing apart from their faith in God to provide them with all they needed. Travelling light, they could move swiftly; carrying no supplies, they were forced to rely on the goodness of others, bringing the gift of charity to the places they visited; without the security of belongings, they found security in God and within themselves, as they saw the wonders that their faith produced: 'On their return the apostles told Jesus all they had done' (Luke 9:10).

As we continue our journey through life, let us pledge to hold lightly to the things we own – enjoying them but not burdened by them, happy to share them with others and always willing to leave them behind if it becomes necessary to do so.

How might you travel more lightly? What things can you do without or would benefit others more than they do you? How can you share the blessings that you have received with those who have less?

SALLY WELCH

Waiting for the right time

A scribe then approached and said, 'Teacher, I will follow you wherever you go.' And Jesus said to him, 'Foxes have holes, and birds of the air have nests; but the Son of Man has nowhere to lay his head.' Another of his disciples said to him, 'Lord, first let me go and bury my father.' But Jesus said to him, 'Follow me, and let the dead bury their own dead.'

My husband is a great journey planner. He loves maps and guidebooks, and at the first indication that I am thinking of making a pilgrimage he will bury his head in the appropriate literature and scour the internet for the best advice on routes and accommodation. In this he is a real blessing, as I have little skill and no interest in this sort of thing. However, very often the journeys we plan will come to nothing – work commitments, the needs of our family and the very effort of planning and carrying out a pilgrimage all conspire to encourage us to do nothing, letting the maps gather dust on the table in the study while we get on with other tasks.

The harshness of Jesus' response to that perfectly sensible request to bury one's father is, I think, based in our natural apathy when it comes to actually getting on and doing what we said we would do. Commentaries have stated that burying one's father does not mean actually attending the funeral of a deceased relative, but instead waiting for the commitment to a family to end in the form of a death that has not yet happened. Jesus tells the scribe that 'now' is a good time – in fact the only time – giving him a sense of urgency about his task and encouraging him to make sure his priorities are the right ones. Sometimes we cannot begin new projects until other commitments have been honoured; at other times these are simply excuses we hide behind in order to avoid stepping out on a new and potentially risky venture.

Lord God, you know the purpose you have for my life.
Help me to discern that purpose and to work towards it.

SALLY WELCH

'You shall also love the stranger'*

Now on that same day two of them were going to a village called Emmaus, about seven miles from Jerusalem, and talking with each other about all these things that had happened. While they were talking and discussing, Jesus himself came near and went with them, but their eyes were kept from recognising him… When he was at the table with them, he took bread, blessed and broke it, and gave it to them. Then their eyes were opened, and they recognised him; and he vanished from their sight. They said to each other, 'Were not our hearts burning within us while he was talking to us on the road, while he was opening the scriptures to us?

One of the gifts of pilgrimage is discovering new travelling companions. A group of strangers who gather to make a pilgrimage together is like a whole stocking full of Christmas gifts – some quirky and funny; some practical and useful; each one chosen with care. The fun of examining each knobbly package, unwrapping it and discovering the contents is paralleled in the surprises that lie hidden in the characters and conversations of those we walk beside.

I have met leaders of industry, poets, priests and waiters on my journeys and have discovered things I never would have expected, both from them and in my response to their experiences. Often I have been shamed by my initial expectations, as an apparently tedious companion has in turn had me both laughing and crying with their anecdotes, reminding me that outward appearances can be deceptive. Just as the hearts of the disciples were 'burning' within them as they spoke to Jesus, so I have learnt great truths from those who have shared the route with me.

Wherever we are, whatever our journeys, there are opportunities for new travelling companions – those we meet in church, at social events, even on hospital visits can become part of our journey experience, offering a rich seam of learning if we are willing to hear their tales and seek the truth that lies within them.

Lord, help me to travel with 'opened eyes'.

SALLY WELCH

* DEUTERONOMY 10:19

Journey companions – meeting with strangers

The Lord appeared to Abraham by the oaks of Mamre, as he sat at the entrance of his tent in the heat of the day. He looked up and saw three men standing near him. When he saw them, he ran from the tent entrance to meet them, and bowed down to the ground. He said, 'My lord, if I find favour with you, do not pass by your servant. Let a little water be brought, and wash your feet, and rest yourselves under the tree. Let me bring a little bread, that you may refresh yourselves, and after that you may pass on – since you have come to your servant.'

This story has been made famous by Rublev's icon of the event. The icon is also said to represent the Trinity, as the Father, Son and Holy Spirit gather round the Communion table, making the shape of a chalice as they do so.

The generosity of Abraham to his guests is rewarded by their prophecy of a child to Sarah, his long-barren wife. It serves as a reminder of the unexpected gifts that strangers seeking hospitality might bring with them – not miracle babies, perhaps, but the opportunity to reach out in love to others, sharing what we have in honour of a God who shared his life and death with us.

We too, in turn, might be in need of hospitality from strangers, and then the art of receiving gracefully and gratefully that which we are offered, accepting gifts as blessings and using them in the best way we can, will become in itself a form of praise to the God who created all things and made us stewards of his bountiful provision.

If you are able, find an illustration of Rublev's beautiful icon painted in 1410 in Russia – either as a postcard or on the internet. Spend some time simply looking at it, exploring its depths and allowing its message to become part of you: 'Glory be to the Father, and to the Son, and to the Holy Spirit, as it was in the beginning, is now and ever shall be, world without end. Amen.'

SALLY WELCH

Travelling with ourselves

But God said to Jonah, 'Is it right for you to be angry about the bush?' And he said, 'Yes, angry enough to die.' Then the Lord said, 'You are concerned about the bush, for which you did not labour and which you did not grow; it came into being in a night and perished in a night. And should I not be concerned about Nineveh, that great city, in which there are more than a hundred and twenty thousand people who do not know their right hand from their left, and also many animals?'

After all that Jonah has been through, he still hasn't quite 'got it'! Furious that the people of Nineveh have listened to his message and repented, thus saving themselves from God's wrath, Jonah spent the previous day sulking under a bush, which has now withered. God, in his infinite tenderness, arranged this lesson to show just how much he cares for his people and how great is his rejoicing when they turn once more towards him. A valuable lesson has been taught, using the natural world as an example – not the first time this has happened and certainly not the last.

The moment we engage with the natural landscape, we see signs of God's care for his creation – in the detail of plants and flowers, the infinite variety of weather conditions, the vast expanse of skies and seas. As we journey, we too become captivated by our surroundings and see our own place within them – and thus God's great love for each one of us.

Many great journeys are undertaken in order to seek healing or understanding or simply to escape – not always successfully. One of the most important lessons we are taught by the road is that wherever we journey we take ourselves with us; our first priority should be to forgive and love ourselves, seeing ourselves as God sees us. It is only then that we will be able to reach out to others and show by our words and actions that they too are infinitely precious to God.

'Come to him, a living stone… chosen and precious in God's sight'
(1 Peter 2:4).

SALLY WELCH

Obstacles on the journey

They will pass through the land, greatly distressed and hungry; when they are hungry, they will be enraged and will curse their king and their gods. They will turn their faces upwards, or they will look to the earth, but will see only distress and darkness, the gloom of anguish; and they will be thrust into thick darkness.

Walking a long way for one day is achievable for almost anyone with a basic level of fitness. Although the final few miles can be tough going, there is usually enough adrenaline in the system to help us through to the end. To get up the following day, stiff and aching, with sore feet and a great weariness, and set off once more can take real courage, as well as a significant amount of effort.

Many people consistently overestimate their level of fitness when planning a long pilgrimage – they do not train hard enough before they set off or they aim to walk an impossibly large number of miles each day. Too often I have seen optimistic walkers striding out at a rapid pace, only to encounter them by the roadside, nursing blisters, tendonitis or similar afflictions. They then have to decide whether to continue on, hoping that their feet and muscles will recover if they adopt a gentler pace, or to stop for a while or altogether.

Unless we are miraculously fortunate, each one of us will encounter physical difficulties to a greater or lesser extent in our lives. Sometimes these are mild or brief enough that they can be weathered fairly easily; at other times their effect is life-altering. The temptation then is to look around for something or someone to blame, to resent the restrictions imposed upon us by our illness and even to take out our anger at our lot on those who share our lives. The struggle and the challenge will be not to 'see only distress and darkness' but to focus on the light – the small signs of improvement; the things we are able still to do; the ways in which we can still positively affect our neighbours and our surroundings.

Lord God, help me to light a candle, not curse the darkness.

SALLY WELCH

Finding out the way

Make me to know your ways, O Lord; teach me your paths. Lead me in your truth, and teach me, for you are the God of my salvation; for you I wait all day long. Be mindful of your mercy, O Lord, and of your steadfast love, for they have been from of old. Do not remember the sins of my youth or my transgressions; according to your steadfast love remember me, for your goodness' sake, O Lord! Good and upright is the Lord; therefore he instructs sinners in the way. He leads the humble in what is right, and teaches the humble his way. All the paths of the Lord are steadfast love and faithfulness, for those who keep his covenant and his decrees.

This is the original pilgrim's psalm for me – short enough to remember, long enough to provide a rhythm to accompany my footsteps. I also use it plentifully when I am standing at the crossroads in the middle of the countryside, staring desperately at a map, trying to decide where to go! To be honest, it is not a lot of help when I am navigating, but it does remind me of the goodness of a God who not only accompanies each one of us on our life's journey, but ensures that our direction and our destination is the right one for us. Wherever we are led by life's events or wherever our own wilful souls may take us, we will find the necessary support and help when we need it.

At the end of a recent discussion held in my church on faith and doubt in the modern world, the speaker reminded us that not only does God meet us on the right path, but he meets us on the wrong path too and gently, lovingly, guides us to our destination. We probably should not start from where we do at times, but God's ways will lead us home.

God of my pilgrimage, help me to be aware of your guiding presence; give me courage as I journey through dark valleys and let me experience the restoration of your peace. May I follow your path and walk in your ways this day and forever.

SALLY WELCH

Resting

Thus the heavens and the earth were finished, and all their multitude. And on the seventh day God finished the work that he had done, and he rested on the seventh day from all the work that he had done. So God blessed the seventh day and hallowed it, because on it God rested from all the work that he had done in creation.

As a parish priest and as a mother and grandmother, there are never enough hours in the day. However early I wake and however continuously I move from task to task, barely pausing for breath, I still cannot get to the end of my to-do list. As soon as one item is checked off, another four are added to the bottom, ensuring that the satisfaction of ticking everything off will never be experienced.

In the early days of my ministry, I did not allow myself to stop and soon learnt the lesson that non-stop working is good for neither vicar nor church community. Now I take seriously the blessing that God gives to our times of rest, following the example that he himself set. No matter how we treat the seven days – literally or metaphorically – the element of rest is an integral part of the process of creation.

So too for us – whether on a physical or a spiritual journey, we must make sure that we give ourselves time to pause and reflect. We can look back on where we have travelled from and set our sight line once more on our destination. We can allow the creative Spirit to fill our souls, stepping aside from the treadmill of busyness to imagine, to dream, to wish, to replenish our vision. Then we will be able to tread the path once more with renewed vigour, approaching our tasks with rested hearts and minds: 'For thus said the Lord God, the Holy One of Israel: In returning and rest you shall be saved; in quietness and in trust shall be your strength' (Isaiah 30:15)

When did you last take a proper time of rest and reflection? When did you last allow yourself space to dream? Is now a good time? If not, when?

SALLY WELCH

Unexpected delights

'Ask, and it will be given to you; search, and you will find; knock, and the door will be opened for you. For everyone who asks receives, and everyone who searches finds, and for everyone who knocks, the door will be opened. Is there anyone among you who, if your child asks for bread, will give a stone? Or if the child asks for a fish, will give a snake? If you then, who are evil, know how to give good gifts to your children, how much more will your Father in heaven give good things to those who ask him!'

Last September I led the children in the Sunday Club on their annual pilgrimage. We focused on experiencing God's creation through our five senses, pausing at various points on the way to see, touch, taste, smell and listen. We ate the plump, juicy blackberries that hung in clumps in the hedgerows lining our path. We listened to the noise of the wind in the leaves of the trees and stared out across the hills, trying to spot the towers of the different churches in the area.

We made slow progress, because using our senses takes time. We made slow progress, because I had given each child a small box and invited them to fill it with as many different objects as they could. The whole party engaged in this activity, offering tiny feathers, acorns, different seed heads or brightly coloured stones to whichever child was nearest, encouraging each to look carefully where they walked, anxious to collect every treasure. We made slow progress, because the event was so precious that we wanted it to last as long as it could, savouring every sun-filled moment, conscious that winter was on the horizon and the bright days might not continue.

The gifts offered to us in our daily journeys are often unexpected and may go unnoticed as we pass by with our eyes on the next task, the next goal. Let us delight in small moments of joy, celebrate gestures of love and friendship, and rejoice in the evidence of God's love, which surrounds us all.

'This is the day that the Lord has made; let us rejoice and be glad in it'
(Psalm 118:24).

SALLY WELCH

The right path

'But while he was still far off, his father saw him and was filled with compassion; he ran and put his arms around him and kissed him. Then the son said to him, "Father, I have sinned against heaven and before you; I am no longer worthy to be called your son." But the father said to his slaves, "Quickly, bring out a robe – the best one – and put it on him; put a ring on his finger and sandals on his feet. And get the fatted calf and kill it, and let us eat and celebrate; for this son of mine was dead and is alive again; he was lost and is found!" And they began to celebrate.'

Route-finding on a pilgrimage is often hugely challenging. Signposts can be missed, paths too overgrown to spot, maps misread. Realising that you have been following the wrong route is depressing – so much energy wasted! But we must retrace our steps so that we can reach our destination, otherwise we will simply stray further afield. It is difficult to do, but vital.

These must have been the thoughts of that heedless young man in Jesus' parable, who had earlier set off so merrily, careless of the feelings of the ones he had left behind. How his mind must have lingered on the comforts of his home as his feet hurried towards that place of solace and ease. He could not be sure of his welcome, so ungrateful had he been, but his resolve to accept his punishment and begin afresh was strong enough to overcome all anxiety and fear. What joy he must have felt when he saw his father and realised that all was forgiven and he was truly home.

As we make our life's journey, we will inevitably wander from the path that leads us home. Fearful of the consequences, we might hesitate to turn again to the right road, afraid that we will no longer be welcome. But our Father, who loves us, forgives us all and will come running to meet us, arms outstretched in his joy at our return.

Lord, lead me in right paths to the true destination.

SALLY WELCH

Pilgrim hearts

'Do not let your hearts be troubled. Believe in God, believe also in me. In my Father's house there are many dwelling-places. If it were not so, would I have told you that I go to prepare a place for you? And if I go and prepare a place for you, I will come again and will take you to myself, so that where I am, there you may be also. And you know the way to the place where I am going.' Thomas said to him, 'Lord, we do not know where you are going. How can we know the way?' Jesus said to him, 'I am the way, and the truth, and the life. No one comes to the Father except through me.'

On reaching a pilgrimage destination, particularly one where the journey has cost a lot of effort and time, the first impulse naturally is to give thanks for the safe arrival. Photographs of grinning pilgrims appear on hundreds of different social media sites and internet searches – weary, scruffy walkers, whose grins reflect the elation of a journey's end.

One of my most poignant mementos of a pilgrimage, however, is a picture of the whole family standing in a cathedral square looking forlorn and sad. We had been so pleased to arrive, and awestruck by the magnificent building that was our destination, but then came the realisation that the adventure was over. No more picnics by riversides or walking through fields and forests. No more sleeping in new places or meeting new people – simply the journey home to the routine of everyday.

Cultivating a pilgrim heart is a precious skill. We must learn to treat every day as an adventure, wherever we find ourselves. We must seek to make friends of strangers and learn new things about familiar companions. We must look with new eyes at well-known landscapes, meeting God in the glories of his creation which surround us. We must journey on, in faith and hope, along the path of righteousness, with Christ as our journey companion and our guide. And always we must hold in our hearts our destination.

'Simon Peter answered him, "Lord, to whom can we go?
You have the words of eternal life"' (John 6:68).

SALLY WELCH

Psalms 15—28

To write about the psalms is no easy assignment. They have such a central place in Christian worship – inspiring hymns, read or chanted with devotion at evensong, quoted in the New Testament at key moments. They are at the core of prayer for many people.

I'll admit I struggle with the psalms at times. The breadth of the emotions they convey means that inevitably it is myself I am struggling with. The fear and desperation they express, or their apparent self-satisfaction, challenge me. Then their peace and their humility touch me deeply. They can be intensely personal, although they come from a context we scarcely know. They can be political and social.

My fondest memories of reading the psalms take me back to evensong as a teenager. We would sing the psalms to Anglican plainchant at the end of the day, my dad beside me. The words of the psalms in the *Book of Common Prayer*, with their coneys, leviathans and unicorns, appealed to my imagination. These words have gone from modern translations, and for the sake of accuracy that is certainly for the best, though a part of me misses them.

At theological college we read the psalms with a short pause between each clause, but without a pause between the sentences. It sounds strange initially, but slows down the reading. Later in a small church in Lincoln I used to join with a couple of parishioners and read evening prayer together in the style we had used at theological college. It was beautifully meditative and simple – we sat on rush-backed chairs, the three of us sharing the readings and keeping our psalm reading at the same pace as one another.

Augustine saw the psalms as a mirror of ourselves. The psalms confront us with ourselves: our fears, faith and rejoicing. Reading the psalms brings us to examine aspects of ourselves and our society that might be painful. They describe God's walk alongside us, our yearning for God's presence and peace. They bring us to address our mortality, our fragility and the shadow that these can threaten to cast over our lives and faith. We need to approach the psalms with humility, recognising that they come from a society very different to our own, but that they can still speak to our very soul.

HARRY SMART

It's only money!

O Lord, who may abide in your tent? Who may dwell on your holy hill? Those who walk blamelessly, and do what is right… who stand by their oath even to their hurt; who do not lend money at interest, and do not take a bribe against the innocent.

The psalms address many different situations – warfare, grand religious ceremonies and personal reflections. It is possible that this psalm originated as a liturgy to be performed by the priest entering the temple. How can he be counted as worthy to perform his duties, to enter the sanctuary?

When I began as a curate, and before, I was nervous about taking services. Leading prayers is a big responsibility, done on behalf of the congregation. Can I find the right words? Will I avoid a subject that needs praying for or phrase something poorly? Am I good enough?

The Israelite priests had similar concerns. Were they good enough to enter such holy premises? What gave them the right to perform their tasks? Perhaps this was read out to the priest as he entered the temple, reminding him of correct behaviour. The first requirements aren't too surprising. The priest should be blameless and truthful. They shouldn't slander others and should do no evil to their friends (15:3). That's quite perceptive – it is my friends who get my sharp edges and fears; I'm not sure I have enemies, really.

The requirements to not 'lend money at interest' and not 'take a bribe against the innocent' come as a surprise. Why include these? In many ways, we are what we do with our money. What we buy says a lot about us. Money gains us education, travel, healthcare and security. That may or may not be just. Money lent or invested unfairly, with concern for our advantage regardless of the exploitation of others and the continuation of injustice, can be hugely divisive and damaging. How often do we include the use of our money in our reflections? Churches have been part of the fair-trade movement for many years, and awareness of our impact on the natural environment is deepening.

This reflection on usury and money is within a book of worship.
Could we include such concerns in our liturgy?

HARRY SMART

A safe place

Protect me, O God, for in you I take refuge. I say to the Lord, 'You are my Lord; I have no good apart from you'… You show me the path of life. In your presence there is fullness of joy.

Think about your best holiday. Or a place that you return to and where you feel happiest. It may be that you have people whom you feel most able to relax with or most able to talk to. Sometimes we need to get away, to return to places where we feel safe or that can hold us.

Many years ago I returned to Iona, where I had been a volunteer some time before. After a long journey and a hard time at work, I was tired. I walked to the North Bay and found a secluded place among the dunes and fell asleep. It was a return home, and I felt safe. Similarly, last year we went to Germany and caught up with friends and relatives and walked along the Danube. It had been a hard year health-wise, and coming back to a country where I felt at ease and walking among the forests and the ancient towns of the region began to restore me.

Both were different times, and I was in a different position, but the sense of homecoming and of restoring my faith and trust was similar. I began to see the beauty of the world around me and the good things of life once again.

Sometimes we lose sight of God's goodness. We can lose sight of goodness around us – we are overwhelmed by the concerns that we have and can feel trapped. We can miss the kindness of people around us, the beauty of the natural world and the simple things.

'I have no good apart from you' need not mean that we discard others. If we see God's goodness in the people and creatures around us, our attitude will be more open. Often retreat houses can be in beautiful parts of the world. Certainly in my experience going on retreat renews my appreciation of the goodness and beauty of life – and that need not be because of the quality of the food!

In you, Lord, I take refuge. Help me to refresh my experience of you.

HARRY SMART

As I am known

If you try my heart, if you visit me by night, if you test me, you will find no wickedness in me; my mouth does not transgress. As for what others do, by the word of your lips I have avoided the ways of the violent. My steps have held fast to your paths.

What keeps you awake at night? Fear of the future? Financial worries? Illness? The psalms are often concerned with reputation. Often people seem to be speaking against the psalmist, making false allegations, and the psalmist is in court fighting for his reputation.

Reputation and honour are precious to many people. How we want to be seen by others is often important. Hopefully, it correlates reasonably closely with some identifiable reality – there is an integrity to our sense of self and what we do. My car, for example, has a Lincolnshire Wildlife Trust sticker on it; I want people to see what sort of person I am and to think about wildlife conservation. Social media does this on a grand scale – most people rarely post about having an ordinary day. Apparently a lot of us are busy doing something worthwhile, exciting or creative. We want to seem interesting, even though our lives are probably as humdrum as most.

But as well as being precious, reputation is also easily damaged. Social media, while being a valuable source of information, can also be used to spread rumours, share information we never intended to reveal or ruin careers without justification.

Jesus warns against doing things for the sake of a public audience (Matthew 6:1–6). He speaks of God knowing what we are doing in secret, so that he might 'reward you'. Prayer and generosity are things to be done quietly, without looking for attention or media coverage. We may not always follow that practice, but it does allow deeper self-knowledge. We aren't depending on the opinion of others to confirm our sense of who we are.

'Guard me as the apple of the eye' (Psalm 17:8). Lord, you know me more deeply than I know myself. I needn't hide myself from you. Help me to trust you and let you hold me in your hand.

HARRY SMART

Which version?

I pursued my enemies and overtook them; and did not turn back until they were consumed. I struck them down, so that they were not able to rise; they fell under my feet. For you girded me with strength for the battle; you made my assailants sink under me. You made my enemies turn their backs to me, and those who hated me I destroyed.

I was singing in a performance of Benjamin Britten's war requiem recently. It sets to music the classic text of the requiem service along with some deeply moving World War I poetry by Wilfred Owen. One of these poems is 'The Parable of the Old Man and the Young', which retells the story of Abraham and Isaac. In the poem, instead of sacrificing the ram caught in the thicket, the old man slaughters Isaac 'and half the seed of Europe, one by one'. There was uncertainty in the choir whether this was the actual Bible story. It's not marked as being by Owen in the musical score. It was only a little later that someone pointed out that this wasn't how the Bible story ends – which increases the horror of the poem's conclusion. It could have been – should have been – different.

The confusion isn't always confined to lack of knowledge of the Bible, though I did find our lack of awareness of the story disturbing. How can we understand the moral point Wilfred Owen was making if we don't know what the original message was – of not sacrificing our children, of being able to step away from our own pride?

Did the writer of the psalm, possibly the king, confuse his own violence with the will of God? Nationalism and religion can be dangerous companions. Together they can excuse racism, violence, war and intolerance. When wars happen, as sadly they will, remembering the humanity and dignity of the enemy is essential if we claim to be inspired by Christ, who spoke of loving our enemies.

How can we remember and celebrate the humanity of others when there is pressure to forget?

HARRY SMART

The voice of creation

The heavens are telling the glory of God; and the firmament proclaims his handiwork. Day to day pours forth speech, and night to night declares knowledge. There is no speech, nor are there words; their voice is not heard.

In the early morning sunlight, I saw a deer cross the woodland path before me. I watched silently and saw another, nervously testing the air, cross as well. But I live near steelworks, so however peaceful it seems the woodland is never silent. The sound of grinding or whistling from the factory, along with the smell of whatever process is happening there, remind me that this is no remote mountainside. The air quality here is a concern for many. Three miles away is a proposed fracking site, which may multiply, bringing more vehicles and encouraging us to use more fossil fuels when we should be striving to use less.

Psalm 19 begins with an overwhelming vision of the exuberance of creation: can we hear creation's voice go 'out through all the earth' (19:4)? Our sense of being under the law of creation, part of it, seems limited, even as we do it and ourselves such harm. The birdsong and the swathes of flowers in the woodland floor speak of lives richer than I know. But the number of insects has dropped by two-thirds in 27 years. This loss of species diminishes creation's voice of praise.

I know I am part of the problem. My car, my whole lifestyle, try as I might, harms God's creation. But perhaps it's better to start with a sense of praise for the beauty of God's creation rather than self-flagellation. In 'Auguries of Innocence', William Blake writes: 'To see a world in a grain of sand and a heaven in a wild flower, hold infinity in the palm of your hand and eternity in an hour.'

Can I live in such a way that I honour God's handiwork?
If I recognise what connects me with creation and live a little more simply,
I may be able to praise God more fully.

HARRY SMART

What I want, what I really, really want!

May he grant you your heart's desire, and fulfil all your plans. May we shout for joy over your victory, and in the name of our God set up our banners. May the Lord fulfil all your petitions.

'What do you want?' is one of those questions that is deceptively simple but takes a lot of consideration. 'What is your heart's desire?' goes deeper, of course – what do you seek at your core? Perhaps it's a question we might feel awkward about answering, like those questionnaires where people say they most want world peace or an end to climate change. Obviously, those are good things to desire, but perhaps they are so idealistic that they seem to excuse us from actually doing anything.

The psalms are all about the search for God. Psalm 42, for example, describes the soul parched and longing for God like a deer for water. Is God what we most desire? What does it mean to say that anyway? 'Where is God in all of this?' is a question often asked by spiritual directors. It can refocus our stories and put things into greater context when we are overwhelmed. Another is 'Where are you in all this?' That's what my spiritual director often asks me when my guy ropes seem to be flapping loose.

What is my heart's desire? Sometimes I get bugged by wanting things – books, clothes, moving house, finding a different job. Those are all legitimate desires, though I can disguise wants as needs – how many tweed jackets or attractive copies of books do I actually need? They are expressions of a desire for beauty and quality and, if bought from fair trade or charity sources at least, for a better way of doing trade.

Which takes us back to God! My life is more than food and my body more than clothes. Those desires aren't bad, but they aren't enough. God goes beyond. Often as I sit doing mindfulness exercises, I am aware of the thoughts going through my head. But sometimes I have a sense of settled peace. That comes close to my heart's desire.

How do we live with our desires and come to know them
and their source better?

HARRY SMART

Victory at any price?

You will destroy their offspring from the earth, and their children from among humankind. If they plan evil against you, if they devise mischief, they will not succeed. For you will put them to flight; you will aim at their faces with your bows.

Many psalms were written for state occasions, and Psalm 21 is dedicated to the king. This may have been David or one of his successors. Celebration of victory was an important communal activity, particularly when the kingdom was surrounded by warlike neighbours, like Egypt and Assyria. Success in warfare was seen as an expression of God's favour; defeat, as punishment for unfaithfulness. In this way Psalm 21 begins with thanksgiving for the length of the king's life and finishes with a description of victory in war.

War may be something that all countries need to be prepared for, at least for immediate self-defence. Countries can define themselves by their military power or warlike history. We in the UK tend to look to World War II as a time when we were on our own against the rest of the world, forgetting the support we received from the Commonwealth countries. But war is a dangerous source of self-definition; it can allow dehumanising behaviour towards enemies. The final verses of Psalm 21 countenance genocide, the wiping out of a nation. Aiming arrows or spears at the faces of the enemy was a way of striking against their personhood.

I have spoken with veterans of World War II. One man drove along the road to Dunkirk ahead of the advancing German troops. His description of what he did and the terror of the beaches at Dunkirk was far from any heroic depiction of war I have ever seen. But he had the courage to be honest about himself to me. He had been caught up in events much bigger than himself, and they haunted him throughout his long life, but he was also hurt by the way his experiences have seldom been acknowledged.

How do we approach war in our churches and in our society?
What stories do we tell, and are we prepared to listen to
the experiences of those on the other side?

HARRY SMART

God doesn't turn away

My God, my God, why have you forsaken me? Why are you so far from helping me, from the words of my groaning? O my God, I cry by day, but you do not answer; and by night, but find no rest.

This is the psalm that Jesus quotes as he hangs on the cross (see Matthew 27:46; Mark 15:34). Suffering can cause us to feel cut off from others, and at times from God too. We don't know what the cause of the psalmist's suffering is – it combines physical illness with shame and the contempt of mockers. Suffering may still be met with moral uncertainty. Why is this person suffering? What have they done to deserve this? Some still see disability as a punishment for something done in a former life.

Many who endure suffering feel isolated. In hospital they are often away from family; people with mental health problems may be many miles away because there aren't enough beds nearby. Medical care is very individualistic – communication can be difficult on a ward, though friendships in shared suffering are tremendously supportive. Illness separates us from our everyday identity; the psalmist feels bitterly alone. The psalmist says he has taken refuge in God since birth; since childhood, faith has been a touchstone. Now all strength has gone: 'I am poured out like water' (22:14). Has that faith been in vain?

I have met many whose faith has been challenged by their suffering but who have also found in their faith a context and relief for their sufferings. Suffering is a condition of humanity – it seems to alienate but it can also draw us closer. Faith goes beyond this feeling of isolation. Psalm 22 keeps faith with God, though it challenges the psalmist. Jesus wasn't forsaken by God, but entered into the deep pain of humanity, and that I'm sure is one reason why the psalm is quoted.

'To him, indeed, shall all who sleep in the earth bow down;
before him shall bow all who go down to the dust, and I shall live for him…
future generations will be told about the Lord' (Psalm 22:29–30). These last
verses of Psalm 22 hint at resurrection – when have you seen that light
despite the darkness?

HARRY SMART

The darkest valley

Even though I walk through the darkest valley, I fear no evil; for you are with me; your rod and your staff – they comfort me. You prepare a table before me in the presence of my enemies.

Psalm 23 is so well known as a hymn that it is near impossible to approach it without many associations. How often have we heard it in the background during deathbed scenes in films? It is often used at funerals, so it is one that should be used sparingly if you are running a singing group in hospital or arranging a service.

Perhaps because of this overfamiliarity, I was reluctant to use Psalm 23 when I was visiting a minister who was dying in hospital. I visited several times over a week, and I knew she enjoyed hearing the psalms read, though she wasn't strong enough to speak much. I avoided using this psalm. It seemed too final, too laden with prior use by us both. But I knew the psalms expressed so much for her throughout the time I had been visiting.

She knew her life was ending. There was an honesty about her and courage that impressed me deeply. She was settled; she was on her last pilgrimage. Psalm 23 is certainly about our mortality – the beauty and peace which we experience is shadowed by the darkest valley. This can be death, but it can be those things that seem to give a foretaste of death, that challenge our sense of identity. Our security is fragile. Psalm 23 asserts our confidence in God and in goodness despite the darkness of the times we live in.

I did read the psalm for her as we gave thanks for all that had spoken of God's presence in her life and all that she had done in her ministry. Doing so felt like a release, a recognition of all that was good, of how God had led her and me in our ministries, and that death couldn't overshadow the fullness of life promised by God to us.

*Can I remember to be aware of my cup overflowing
even when times may be dark?*

HARRY SMART

The well is deep

The earth is the Lord's and all that is in it, the world, and those who live in it; for he has founded it on the seas, and established it on the rivers.

Many years ago on a holiday on South Uist in the Outer Hebrides, we met an elderly lady drawing water from a very plain well in the ground with a plastic bucket. Her grandfather had dug the well and, apart from a few years when she had worked as a herring girl, she had lived in that house all her life. She spoke with passion about her well – it connected her back to her ancestors, to the building of the house and to the natural world around her. It was just a hole in the ground, but went deep into the earth and was dug by hand.

We've lost connection with where our water comes from. It's essential for us, bringing life wherever it is. Think of how many animals will be attracted into a garden by a pond. But we take it for granted, pollute it, use it for disposal of our rubbish. Many churches are built near wells or springs, perhaps because they were already sacred sites, but also I'm sure because those early Christians wanted to honour water and its creator. In most churches the font is at the entrance, sometimes bathed in light from the surrounding windows, and originally the water for baptism would have come from a local well.

Water is used as a symbol of restoration and healing. Chester Cathedral has a beautiful fountain, depicting Jesus receiving water from the woman of Samaria at the well. Jesus asks the woman for water and speaks of himself as living water. In the statue the bowl, held by both figures, overflows with water. It is a wonderfully peaceful, refreshing place. The cloisters had been the site of the original Benedictine well.

Water brings life, but it's not just for humans. The woman of Samaria tells us that both Jacob's sons and his flocks used the well that Jesus drinks from. All of life requires water. Jesus as the living water is also the source of creation.

How can I celebrate life-giving water in my life?

HARRY SMART

Loneliness

Turn to me and be gracious to me, for I am lonely and afflicted. Relieve the troubles of my heart, and bring me out of my distress. Consider my affliction and my trouble, and forgive all my sins.

Loneliness is on the rise. Many of the patients I visit are lonely – family may live far away or be separated from their friends and communities. Loneliness certainly afflicts older people, but it is young people who seem to be experiencing it more than anyone else. In a world in which we can communicate in so many ways, we miss the sound and contact of people we love.

Loneliness exacerbates health problems and leads to anxiety and mental ill-health. Some of the most important conversations I've had recently in hospital have been about local walks, favourite books and Minis (the original designs), rather than about illness or religion. We need to be recognised as humans with all our aspects.

Outside hospital it's similar. A charity encourages friends to phone one another rather than to text – it's good to hear a voice. We are urged to ask twice how someone is, to get past the automatic response of 'I'm okay.' Work does not always offer opportunities for socialising. And while you can video call a friend on the other side of the world, you can't share lunch with them. For old and young alike, feelings of shame or inadequacy can contribute to the feeling of isolation.

Psalm 25 addresses this clearly. The psalmist feels guilty and ashamed, needing acceptance and forgiveness. Past mistakes and failure plague him, and he asks for them to be forgotten by God. Although he speaks of God as loving those who keep his covenant, the psalmist is aware that he has a history that may not have been quite so clear cut.

Jesus ate with his friends and welcomed newcomers too – think of the sinful woman entering Simon's house (Luke 7:36–50). Our churches can be places of welcome.

Was there a moment when you felt on the outside and were made welcome?

HARRY SMART

Breathing and walking

But as for me, I walk in my integrity; redeem me, and be gracious to me. My foot stands on level ground; in the great congregation I will bless the Lord.

The psalms can be a rocky ride. We can go from despair and self-loathing to serenity and confidence. In this psalm, the writer appears to have reached a state of equilibrium.

Every morning I spend ten minutes sitting still, breathing and just being. I'm practising mindfulness, which feels like holding myself before God, breathing, as God breathed into his creation. Hildegard of Bingen wrote of being a 'feather on the breath of God'. This gives a lovely sense of lightness and fragility. It inspired her to see God in the greenness of creation, the imminence of the divine presence. It gave her the courage to challenge popes and emperors.

There's a real interest in mindfulness among nursing staff. In an environment that places great demands on them – from patients, colleagues and the institution – many staff feel the need to find some stillness and look beyond the superficial. It's an opportunity for release for people who are always on the go. But it also helps with their work – on a busy ward there can be many demands on attention. Focusing for a moment allows them not to be overwhelmed by the different needs that surround them.

Several years ago, I ran a spirituality group with people with mental health problems. We unrolled a long strip of wallpaper on the lawn and coloured our feet with paint. Then each of us walked on the wallpaper. Each footstep was done consciously and with consideration.

It's hard to be true to oneself with all of life's demands. I try to do a couple of sessions of mindfulness every day. It takes work – shouldn't I be making the coffee or the porridge? But for those minutes I can be present and just breathe. YHWH, the name of God, is partly understood as the breath of God, fundamental to all life and closer than anything else.

Take five minutes without TV or computer, and just breathe.
How does it feel?

HARRY SMART

The search for God

Hear, O Lord, when I cry aloud, be gracious to me and answer me! 'Come,' my heart says, 'seek his face!' Your face, Lord, do I seek. Do not hide your face from me.

'Now we see in a mirror, dimly,' writes the apostle Paul, 'but then we will see face to face' (1 Corinthians 13:12). The psalms are a search for God. At the moments of greatest solemnity – entering the temple, in war, times of uncertainty and fear – the search is for God even when the psalmist feels abandoned.

Augustine, in his *Confessions*, writes that 'our hearts are restless till they find their rest in you'. The book is an account of Augustine's life and the thread of God that works through his story. He often falls short, gets distracted or takes what might be a wrong turn, but everything is told in the context of that journey or search towards God.

The search for closeness to God, to the core of our being, is inherent, but not always clear. This was conveyed to me in a labyrinth-walking group as some women explored the effort it took going out of the front door. 'Do I look okay? What if something goes wrong? What if I get hurt?' But then I think of some of those people who have had bad news, such as that their illness is terminal, and approach it with quiet faith and trust in God. It's not a denial, but an acceptance and sense that they are returning home.

Psalm 27 begins, 'The Lord is my light… whom shall I fear?' I am quite often afraid, especially about my health and my work. Did I get this or that right? The psalm acknowledges that we do get afraid; we fear to lose God's face. The language of seeking can put too much onus on us to act, when all the time God is in fact seeking us!

When do we feel closer to God, and when are we searching?

HARRY SMART

Redemption song

Hear the voice of my supplication, as I cry to you for help, as I lift up my hands towards your most holy sanctuary. Do not drag me away with the wicked, with those who are workers of evil, who speak peace with their neighbours, while mischief is in their hearts.

The psalmist is in despair, calling out to God. It may be the king himself who is speaking; certainly he feels close enough to the temple to appeal to the holy sanctuary, the most sacred part of the temple. The speaker is looking for a touchstone, a point of stability, when everything else is becoming insecure. Treachery is rife.

Whoever these people are, they are workers of evil who betray their neighbours while claiming to speak peace. Terrible things can happen when trust is broken within society. It has happened within so many countries in the last century – think of East Germany or Rwanda. The wounds of such divisions take years to heal. In the psalm, people seem to have forgotten the things God has done. They don't see his work. They can't see what is good. Many of the later psalms recount the events of Israel's history: Psalm 78 is a history of not recognising God's actions; Psalm 105 reminds the hearers of Jacob, Moses and Aaron, sent to recover the people from famine and oppression.

In a time of division and mistrust, to tell stories together and recover a sense of identity that can foster harmony and peace between communities becomes essential. Without it the psalmist himself is afraid that he too will be taken away, overthrown or arrested. However, the final verses of the psalm indicate that something has changed: stability has been recovered. 'O save your people, and bless your heritage,' pleads the psalmist (28:9). The psalmist is asking for a clearer sense of self for the people, sustained by faith in God, who is a shepherd caring for and sustaining his people forever. This is a vision of God not as dictator coming to impose order, but as one who knows us all and who calls us to be part of his kingdom unfolding across history.

How can the church be a source of reconciliation and trust in our society?

HARRY SMART

Judges 13—21

'Desperate.' 'Grim.' 'Repulsive.' These are some of the responses from Christian friends when they discovered the passages chosen for these studies. If the Bible is the word of God, what is the purpose of these final chapters of the book of Judges? The accounts of lying, deceit, idolatry, torture, family breakdown, rape, mass murder and other actions depict the worst of humanity. How are we intended to read them?

There are no positive role models in Judges 13—21. Samson is almost a parody of leadership, and there are grotesque and comedic elements in his adventures. The lesser-known Micah makes a silver idol and hires a priest, only to have both taken from him by the tribe of Dan, seeking somewhere to call home. The story of the unnamed Levite, whose concubine is gang-raped before being dismembered, is told so that the unspeakable horror of the events is powerfully conveyed. Finally, the revenge of God's people against the tribe of Benjamin apparently lacks any mercy or proportion: even when a remnant is spared, women are kidnapped and raped for the family line to be preserved.

Yet in any given month, the world news shows every aspect of life alluded to in these chapters. Perhaps we need to not simply consider the accounts but more importantly notice our own responses to the passages. We might ask questions of our God, who apparently permits violence. At the same time we can be aware of our own thinking about right and wrong in difficult times, living with opposing cultures. What can these stories tell us about how to interpret God's calling and purpose alongside feelings of fear, anger and defensiveness? Where is the God and Father of our Lord Jesus Christ among all the other 'gods'?

Finally, although 'in those days there was no king [and] all the people did what was right in their own eyes' (Judges 21:25), Christians have been set free by the King of kings. You might take an hour to read through all the chapters before looking at the individual studies. As you do so, guided by the Holy Spirit, may you each day discern God's sovereignty, discover God's kingdom and experience God's peace, whatever your circumstances.

LAKSHMI JEFFREYS

Dedicated to God

The angel of the Lord appeared to the woman and said to her, 'Although you are barren, having borne no children, you shall conceive and bear a son. Now be careful not to drink wine or strong drink, or to eat anything unclean, for you shall conceive and bear a son. No razor is to come on his head, for the boy shall be a nazirite to God from birth. It is he who shall begin to deliver Israel from the hand of the Philistines.'

Once the Israelites were established in the promised land, they regularly forgot God's laws. Then, when they were oppressed by their enemies and crying out to the Lord, God would choose a 'judge' (civil or military leader) through whom God would rescue his people. At this point in history, God had allowed the Philistines to rule for 40 years, and the people were desperate. But God's solution was different from previously appointed judges: an angel came to Samson's barren parents, telling them that their son, dedicated to God, would deliver God's people.

There is a theme in the Bible of formerly childless couples being told by angels that their longed-for baby will grow up to lead God's people. In the New Testament, Zechariah and Elizabeth are told of the birth of John the Baptist only a few months before an angel appears to the teenage Mary. Samson is one of God's people, whose vocation is specified before he is born and whose parents do all they can to obey God's instructions.

Following Jesus' life, death and resurrection, all of us are invited to 'work out your own salvation with fear and trembling' (Philippians 2:12) within the context of God's people. Whether we have been 'born again' on a specific occasion or we have gradually become aware of belonging to the household of faith, each of us has a vocation (calling) as a disciple of Jesus. Regardless of the context, we are responsible to God not only for living lives holy and pleasing to God, but also for enabling our sisters and brothers in Christ to flourish in their discipleship.

Thank God for those whose Christian vocation has enabled you to flourish.
Pray for people whom you can encourage in discipleship.

LAKSHMI JEFFREYS

Experiencing God

The angel of the Lord did not appear again to Manoah and his wife. Then Manoah realised that it was the angel of the Lord. And Manoah said to his wife, 'We shall surely die, for we have seen God.' But his wife said to him, 'If the Lord had meant to kill us, he would not have accepted a burnt-offering and a grain-offering at our hands, or shown us all these things, or now announced to us such things as these.'

Manoah's wife recognises that the angel was sent from God and simply accepts what he says. Meanwhile Manoah is desperate for a personal encounter. When the angel makes his speech to the couple together, Manoah, understandably, wants to honour the man of God, first with hospitality and then to thank him by name when the baby arrives. The angel explains that any glory is to be given to God. So Manoah and his wife prepare an offering. As it burns, the angel ascends in the flame and, seeing this, the couple fall on their faces. This indeed is holy territory.

When the angel speaks to Manoah's wife, he does not need to insert 'Do not be afraid' into the message. I find it fascinating that it is the unnamed woman who initially sees the angel on both the occasions he appears; she is in awe but her belief in the messenger and message seems unquestioning. This is possibly the basis of her sensible comment as her husband panics: if God has made these promises, he's hardly likely to destroy us!

There can be enormous pressure today to encounter the Holy Spirit such that we have supernatural experiences. Maybe angels, God's messengers, more often speak words of peace and hope from the living God than perform dramatic signs. Throughout the Bible, when God has been revealed in remarkable ways, it is usually shortly before or after something scary and life-changing. We are called to walk daily by faith, not by sight. Any occurrences that cause us to give glory to God along the way are necessary gifts, whether supernatural or otherwise.

Consider the different reactions of Manoah and his wife to the angel. What is your attitude to spiritual encounters?

LAKSHMI JEFFREYS

God's chosen leader

At Timnah [Samson] saw a Philistine woman… and told his father and mother, 'I saw a Philistine woman at Timnah; now get her for me as my wife.' But his father and mother said to him, 'Is there not a woman among your kin, or among all our people, that you must go to take a wife from the uncircumcised Philistines?' But Samson said to his father, 'Get her for me, because she pleases me.' His father and mother did not know that this was from the Lord.

Samson's parents were devout. As a result their son grew and was blessed so that God's Spirit stirred in him (Judges 13:24–25). What a shock, then, to meet the adult Samson: not a pious warrior but a brash, discourteous young man. Samson apparently disregards God's laws concerning marrying a foreign woman (here one of his people's oppressors) and shows no respect towards his parents when they try to dissuade him. When Samson and his parents go to Timnah, God's Spirit rushes on Samson and, unbeknown to his parents, he kills a lion with his bare hands and later eats honey from bees in the carcass. (He blatantly ignores his Nazirite vows, touching and even eating something from a dead body.) We are told that Samson's demand to marry a Philistine and his subsequent actions were 'from the Lord'. Yet how can such an unholy person be God's chosen saviour?

History is littered with Christian leaders whose lifestyles are at odds with their positions of trust and responsibility. As we shall see with Samson, all sin has consequences for the sinner and those around them. It is heartbreaking to meet people whose lives have been blighted by Christians whose actions have been careless, shameful or worse. Thankfully the crucified and risen Jesus shows that even death has no bounds for God's mercy and grace, and good can result from the worst behaviour.

Our role is not to pass judgement on other people but to be accountable for our own words and actions, repenting and seeking forgiveness when necessary and praying daily for grace to grow the fruit of the Spirit.

Read James 4, then hold before God yourself and Christians
with any leadership role.

LAKSHMI JEFFREYS

True to form

Samson's wife wept before him, saying, 'You hate me; you do not really love me. You have asked a riddle of my people, but you have not explained it to me.' He said to her, 'Look, I have not told my father or my mother. Why should I tell you?' She wept before him for the seven days that their feast lasted; and because she nagged him, on the seventh day he told her.

At the time of his wedding, Samson sets a riddle for his Philistine peers. If they explain it properly he will pay them; if not, they are to pay him. The young men threaten Samson's wife; she in turn nags Samson until he enlightens her. The young men correctly answer the riddle, so in a rage Samson kills 30 other young men in order to settle his debt and then abandons his new wife.

In one way the angel's words to Samson's parents are being fulfilled: Samson kills increasingly large groups of Philistines and destroys their livelihoods as God's Spirit comes upon him. God works through Samson's selfishness and impetuosity to gradually destroy the enemies of God's people. At the same time, Samson seems to typify God's people, especially in the Old Testament, as he assimilates with those outside the faith while working, at least nominally, for God. (We shall see this increasingly in later studies.)

Samson remains true to form, in his case allowing his passions to overcome his vocation. Christians, on the other hand, are those whose natural way of being can be realigned to God's original intention for us. When we are increasingly transformed by the Holy Spirit into the likeness of Jesus, we shall discover how to work through our passions to fulfil our true vocation. As noted earlier, our vocation is to grow in discipleship, increasingly knowing Jesus and becoming like him. This happens as we seek to love God with heart, soul, mind and strength and to love our neighbours as ourselves. It takes a lifetime of prayer, practice and forgiveness.

Spend some time discerning how God uses your strengths and weaknesses. (You might find it helpful to talk to a wise Christian friend.) Then pray as God leads you.

LAKSHMI JEFFREYS

Glory and honour

By then [Samson] was very thirsty, and he called on the Lord, saying, 'You have granted this great victory by the hand of your servant. Am I now to die of thirst, and fall into the hands of the uncircumcised?' So God split open the hollow place that is at Lehi, and water came from it. When he drank, his spirit returned, and he revived. Therefore it was named En-hakkore, which is at Lehi to this day. And he judged Israel in the days of the Philistines for twenty years.

Samson's wife is given to another man, so Samson destroys the Philistines' crops. The Philistines, in turn, burn Samson's wife and her father. Samson swears revenge on the Philistines, kills more of them, is handed over to the enemy by his own people and finally kills a thousand Philistines using a donkey's jawbone. (Again Samson breaks his Nazirite vow, touching a corpse.) The story moves from humorous to grotesque with almost cartoon-like violence. Judges 15 portrays the Philistines as ridiculous figures and God's people as pathetic.

Samson is definitely the hero, yet he remains as arrogant as ever. He calls on God, acknowledging that God gave Samson victory over the Philistines, but with a lack of reverence. He demands a drink (reminiscent of God's people in the wilderness under Moses' leadership), claiming he is dying. Once revived, Samson begins his role of judge and the place where the water came is named En-hakkore, traditionally translated 'the spring of the one who called out'. In other words, Samson is honoured for calling out to God, rather than God for providing water.

It is easy to ask God to bless our plans and then to take credit ourselves. A famous Christian author speaks of the danger of 'believing your own publicity'. He has two antidotes: first, he listens to people who love him dearly but who simultaneously act as his harshest critics, reminding him of what he is like away from the public gaze; second, he spends time serving people with learning difficulties who respond not to achievement but to genuine kindness.

'The Son of Man came not to be served but to serve,
and to give his life a ransom for many' (Matthew 20:28).

LAKSHMI JEFFREYS

A joke

Samson went to Gaza, where he saw a prostitute and went in to her. The Gazites were told, 'Samson has come here.' So they encircled the place and lay in wait for him all night at the city gate. They kept quiet all night, thinking, 'Let us wait until the light of the morning; then we will kill him.' But Samson lay only until midnight. Then at midnight he rose up, took hold of the doors of the city gate and the two posts, pulled them up, bar and all, put them on his shoulders, and carried them to the top of the hill that is in front of Hebron.

As we shall see, Samson's downfall is his desire for women. Following his short-lived marriage and its aftermath, Samson chooses sex without ongoing relationship, visiting a prostitute in Gaza. What follows is a joke, pure and simple: in order to escape the people of Gaza, out to capture him, Samson pulls off the doors of the city gates and runs away with them. Samson's enemies lose all credibility and, on this occasion, Samson and the people of God triumph. While there is not much to laugh at for God's people under Philistine rule, it is easy to imagine them chuckling for years to come over this episode!

Although not necessarily the point of the story, I am reminded that even in the most terrifying situations, we do well to discern what is really serious and, if possible, to laugh at the rest. Brian Keenan was a hostage in Beirut and subjected to solitary confinement and torture before being in a cell with other captives. Recalling times he spent laughing with fellow prisoners, he later wrote: 'There are many things a man can resist – pain, torture, loss of loved ones – but laughter ultimately he cannot resist' (*An Evil Cradling*, Vintage, 1993, p. 269). In a less significant way, when circumstances become rather more intense than necessary, I have started to add 'gate' to the possible area of conflict. This has meant managing, among other things, 'land-gate', 'tree-gate', 'toilet-gate' and 'homework-gate'. (Please use your imagination!)

Gracious God, thank you for comic moments, even in tragic
or frightening times. Teach us to trust you and to learn to laugh.

LAKSHMI JEFFREYS

Dangerous liaisons (1)

After this [Samson] fell in love with a woman in the valley of Sorek, whose name was Delilah. The lords of the Philistines came to her and said to her, 'Coax him, and find out what makes his strength so great, and how we may overpower him, so that we may bind him in order to subdue him; and we will each give you eleven hundred pieces of silver.' So Delilah said to Samson, 'Please tell me what makes your strength so great, and how you could be bound, so that one could subdue you.'

Theologians surmise that the book of Judges was written for God's people in exile, centuries later, as they tried to make sense of what had happened to them. Much of the Old Testament shows the folly of becoming so entwined with the prevailing culture that God's people lose their first love for the living God, who has saved them on so many previous occasions.

Samson continues to be driven by his emotions and falls in love with Delilah. He has learned nothing from his previous liaisons with local women, who showed their allegiance to their Philistine people above any feelings for Samson. On three separate occasions, Delilah betrays Samson for money. Knowing the story in context, it is hard to work out why Samson stays with a scheming woman who is plotting his downfall. It could not be clearer, to us at least, that Delilah does not care for Samson.

The Message suggests that Christians should not 'become so well-adjusted to your culture that you fit into it without even thinking. Instead, fix your attention on God. You'll be changed from the inside out. Readily recognise what he wants from you, and quickly respond to it. Unlike the culture around you, always dragging you down to its level of immaturity, God brings the best out of you' (Romans 12:2).

In the early church, Christians used to fast on Wednesdays and Fridays. By taking control in one area of life in order to focus on God, they would allow God to become the primary focus in other areas of life and not be subsumed into the surrounding culture.

How can you become countercultural for Christ?

LAKSHMI JEFFREYS

Dangerous liaisons (2)

Then [Delilah] said, 'The Philistines are upon you, Samson!' When he awoke from his sleep, he thought, 'I will go out as at other times, and shake myself free.' But he did not know that the Lord had left him. So the Philistines seized him and gouged out his eyes. They brought him down to Gaza and bound him with bronze shackles; and he ground at the mill in the prison. But the hair of his head began to grow again after it had been shaved.

Yesterday we considered how Samson was unable to see what was going on with Delilah. Blind to Delilah's scheming and to God's ways, Samson is now literally blinded – the Philistines gouge out his eyes. Appointed before his birth as God's chosen leader, Samson has allowed his appetites to dictate his way through life and has ignored the discipline of the message of the angel to his parents. He now pays the price of his folly.

One of the most sobering statements of the Bible is the phrase, 'But he did not know that the Lord had left him'. In the past we have seen how God's Spirit came on Samson and how Samson's strength, cunning and emotions were used to bring about God's will. Throughout his life it is as if Samson has taken God's presence for granted, assuming that God will bless him whatever he does. Unfortunately for Samson (and for all who take for granted their relationship with God) this is never the case.

Consider the Christian who, over time, stops praying and reading the Bible; who increasingly makes excuses to avoid people and activities that would allow them to be accountable for their actions. When tragedy strikes or serious temptation arises, that person moves further from the Christian community and from God. It is as if they have an image of God as a taskmaster or in some other way not on their side. At some level they might expect condemnation instead of loving forgiveness and support from the church. Only today I heard about a couple who are choosing to struggle on their own rather than allowing Jesus, through his body, the church, to walk with them.

'If we are faithless, he remains faithful – for he cannot deny himself'
(2 Timothy 2:13).

LAKSHMI JEFFREYS

Hero of faith

Then Samson called to the Lord and said, 'Lord God, remember me and strengthen me only this once, O God, so that with this one act of revenge I may pay back the Philistines for my two eyes.' And Samson grasped the two middle pillars on which the house rested, and he leaned his weight against them, his right hand on the one and his left hand on the other. Then Samson said, 'Let me die with the Philistines.'

After Samson's many failures, it seems odd that he is listed as a hero of faith in Hebrews 11:32. Even in death, Samson is not thinking about God's people, whom he was called to serve. When he calls to God for revenge on the enemy, it is not because of their 40 years of oppression but because they blinded him. Samson remains self-centred to the end, yet the writer of Hebrews names him alongside Abraham, Moses, David, Samuel and others who, although they were not perfect, listened to God. Perhaps Samson is a hero because God clearly worked through Samson's strengths and weaknesses. Ultimately Samson's heroism is not his but God's.

God's plan regularly comes about through the leader who suffers. Submitting to God means that Christians are faithful through suffering, enabling God to work through them. God the Father suffered as Jesus suffered on the cross. God worked through suffering and death and brought resurrection and new life. Where Christian leaders have shared the suffering of the people around them, thereby suffering with God, miraculous peace and hope have followed.

Church leaders in South Africa were tortured and martyred when they spoke out against apartheid. Following the abolition of apartheid, Christians called for reconciliation rather than revenge. The elections in 1994 took place more peacefully than anyone could have imagined – a modern miracle. Perhaps Samson is a hero because he recognised his need for God's help in the midst of suffering; God then used Samson's suffering and death to bring about God's good purposes.

God used Samson's strength but achieved more through his weakness. What might have happened had Samson submitted to God? Can you submit to God in suffering and in strength?

LAKSHMI JEFFREYS

Worship

There was a man in the hill country of Ephraim whose name was Micah… His mother took two hundred pieces of silver, and gave it to the silversmith, who made it into an idol of cast metal; and it was in the house of Micah. This man Micah had a shrine, and he made an ephod and teraphim… Then Micah said, 'Now I know that the Lord will prosper me, because the Levite has become my priest.'

Judges 17 introduces new characters. Micah has stolen 1,100 pieces of silver from his mother but returns it on hearing that she has cursed the thief. (Does she suspect her son?) His mother consecrates the restored money to the Lord, then gives her son 200 pieces with which to make two idols. (What happened to the remaining 900 consecrated silver pieces?)

Micah installs one of his sons as a priest until he sees an unemployed young Levite. (Levites, the priestly tribe, were not allocated land. Instead the other tribes were instructed to provide for them in exchange for which the Levite priests would undertake correct forms of worship.) Micah offers the young man food, money and clothes if he will be the priest for Micah's household; the Levite agrees and is treated as one of the family. Micah feels blessed indeed.

The story has an ominous tone: 'In those days there was no king in Israel; all the people did what was right in their own eyes' (17:6). Micah has been portrayed as a thief and as scared of his mother and her curses. In other respects, he appears to be acting as well as he is able, albeit doing what is right in his eyes. He wants the Lord to prosper him – and who doesn't?

Opinion is divided as to whether Micah deliberately ignored the commandment not to make idols or whether he was worshipping God in the only way he knew. Today many people are spiritually hungry but not interested in 'organised religion'. Maybe Christians need to listen to people before criticising their worship, and then introduce Jesus, in whom all their hunger is satisfied.

Paul in Athens used a shrine to 'an unknown God' to speak about Jesus (see Acts 17:23).

LAKSHMI JEFFREYS

In the name of God?

The Danites, having taken what Micah had made, and the priest who belonged to him, came to Laish, to a people quiet and unsuspecting, put them to the sword, and burned down the city... They rebuilt the city, and... named the city Dan... Then the Danites set up the idol for themselves... So they maintained as their own Micah's idol that he had made, as long as the house of God was at Shiloh.

Spies from the tribe of Dan are seeking land when they meet Micah's priest. He tells them they are on a mission from the Lord. The spies discover that the nearby land of Laish is fertile and the current occupants peaceful. Returning with the rest of the tribe, they appropriate Micah's two silver idols. The Levite tries to stop them but the Danites strongly encourage the Levite to be their priest. Micah objects but, realising 600 Danites against one Ephraimite are not good odds, he relinquishes the idols and the priest. Our passage tells how they annihilate the inhabitants of Laish and take the land for their own. An additional detail is that the priest is Jonathan, the grandson of Moses. His family remain priests to the Danites until the exile of God's people.

Mass murder, acquisition of land and property by force and assimilating various forms of worship, all in the name of the living God, have taken place throughout history. 'Holy wars' are not restricted to any individual religion. At the time of writing, the news contains items about the persecution of Christians in one country while a different land tries to extricate itself from the legacy of Christian missionaries whose behaviour did not demonstrate the fruit of the Spirit. The tribe of Dan received God's blessing from the Levite but the people of Laish were destroyed. How can this be the will of the God of love? Ethical questions do not have easy answers, but it is important to wrestle in prayer and discussion before coming to a (temporary) conclusion about what is right or wrong.

Consider the words of Oliver Cromwell: 'I beseech you, in the bowels of Christ, think it possible that you may be mistaken.'

LAKSHMI JEFFREYS

The worst of humanity

When he had entered his house, he took a knife, and grasping his concubine he cut her into twelve pieces, limb by limb, and sent her throughout all the territory of Israel. Then he commanded the men whom he sent, saying, 'Thus shall you say to all the Israelites, "Has such a thing ever happened since the day that the Israelites came up from the land of Egypt until this day? Consider it, take counsel, and speak out."'

Read the whole of Judges 19 and you will find no 'wholesome' individuals. The concubine runs away from the Levite to her father's home. Four months later the Levite pursues her with a view to 'speak tenderly to her' (19:3). As it turns out, he and the concubine's father spend time together, and the concubine is not mentioned. The Levite is persuaded to stay. Eventually after five days, the Levite and concubine journey home, stopping in Gibeah overnight. Initially not offered any local hospitality, an old man from Ephraim takes them in. Men of Gibeah surround the house and demand sex with the Levite. Instead the Levite throws out his concubine to the men, who rape her all night and leave her. At dawn she collapses on the threshold of the house, where the Levite finds her, tosses her on a donkey and takes her home.

The Levite's subsequent actions are recounted in today's passage. His priority is to ensure that he is not blamed for anything: when questioned by the tribal leaders to whom he sent the concubine's dismembered body, his account of events suggests the woman died as a result of the rape, omitting that the Levite threw her out in the first place and did not care for her afterwards (20:4–6). This is an appalling way to live: without reference to God, where power, selfishness, pride and violence have no limits.

Across the world women and girls continue to be victims of sexual violence, whether in domestic settings or in military conflicts where gang rape of civilians is recognised as a war crime. Surely the role of the church must be to 'consider it, take counsel, and speak out'.

May we repent and turn back to Christ. Lord, have mercy.

LAKSHMI JEFFREYS

Family breakdown

Then all the Israelites… went back to Bethel and wept, sitting there before the Lord; they fasted that day until evening. Then they offered burnt-offerings and sacrifices of well-being before the Lord. And the Israelites inquired of the Lord (for the ark of the covenant of God was there in those days, and Phinehas son of Eleazar, son of Aaron, ministered before it in those days), saying, 'Shall we go out once more to battle against our kinsfolk the Benjaminites, or shall we desist?' The Lord answered, 'Go up, for tomorrow I will give them into your hand.'

God's people, the Israelites, are horrified at what has happened. The men of Gibeah are members of the tribe of Benjamin, so leaders of the other tribes go to their brothers from Benjamin and ask them to hand over the criminals. The Benjaminites refuse to listen to 'their kinsfolk, the Israelites' (20:13) and instead come from Gibeah and beyond in their thousands to wage war against the rest of God's people. The Benjaminites win the first two battles, despite the Israelites having consulted the Lord prior to each conflict. Understandably devastated, the Israelites come before the Lord with fasting and tears to discover what to do next. It appears that God's response is that there has to be more armed conflict within the family.

Victory comes only after the people fast and pray, acknowledging that they have not always sought God's way. After all that has happened, perhaps the whole of God's people needed to learn humility before God. Eventually they destroy the Benjaminites, except for 600 men who escape into the wilderness.

The church is the body of Christ (1 Corinthians 12:12–31; Ephesians 4), and when one part suffers, the whole body suffers. The history of God's church is peppered with schism and disagreement. Often God will gradually redeem the situation, but there is always a cost, both within the church and beyond.

'Maintain the unity of the Spirit in the bond of peace.
There is one body and one Spirit… one Lord, one faith,
one baptism, one God and Father of all' (Ephesians 4:3–6).
Ask God to bless other Christians with whom you disagree.

LAKSHMI JEFFREYS

Right in whose eyes?

'What shall we do for wives for those who are left, since we have sworn by the Lord that we will not give them any of our daughters as wives?'... The Benjaminites... took wives for each of them from the dancers whom they abducted... So the Israelites departed from there at that time by tribes and families, and they went out from there to their own territories. In those days there was no king in Israel; all the people did what was right in their own eyes.

Judges 21 is a sorry tale of excessive violence leading to more violence. The people of God do not want the tribe of Benjamin to die out, but they will not allow their own daughters to intermarry with them. So they capture 400 young women from Jabesh-gilead and kill all the other men, women and children. There are still not sufficient wives for the 600 Benjaminites, so the daughters of Shiloh, dancing at an annual religious festival, pay the price.

The whole of the book of Judges is neatly summarised at the end: the people did what they thought or felt was right rather than being directed by God. The irony is that even when kings were appointed, God's way was not always followed. In fact, the human desire to do what is right in our own eyes, rather than seeking God's way, accounts for almost every problem in the world throughout history.

The apostle Paul summarises the human dilemma: 'I decide to do good, but I don't *really* do it; I decide not to do bad, but then I do it anyway. My decisions, such as they are, don't result in actions... I've tried everything and nothing helps... Is there no one who can do anything for me?... The answer, thank God, is that Jesus Christ can and does' (Romans 7:19–25, MSG).

Jesus' death and resurrection allow us to be forgiven and restored every time we see through our eyes rather than God's. Perhaps the book of Judges reminds us of the need for God's Holy Spirit to transform us, not simply as individuals but as the people of God.

Come, Holy Spirit.

LAKSHMI JEFFREYS

Acts 9—11

For the next couple of weeks, we're plunging into the middle of the book of Acts – and the surging energy of those chapters is at times as breathtaking as diving into cold water. In Acts 9—11, we're in the post-Pentecost era, and the young church's growth is rapid (almost) beyond belief. The Spirit has come, and he is moving unstoppably.

We see not only spiritual energy at work but also a lot of physical energy: Saul travels to Damascus, to Jerusalem, then home to Tarsus, and he finally arrives in Antioch; Peter 'travels about the country' as far as the coast; we hear of people spreading the gospel as far as Cyprus. Repeatedly Luke, the author of Acts, tells us of people 'getting up' and 'starting out' – and it's easy to forget that this wasn't a matter of simply starting the car or jumping on a train. Travel was arduous, time-consuming and occasionally dangerous, but God's power was literally putting believers on their feet and on the road, to share the good news.

If we have been blessed to live in such a springtime season, perhaps in our own local church, we will always remember the excitement and the anticipation of what God might do next. As is the way of seasons, though, they pass and for too many congregations (and individuals), 'springtime in the church' is a distant memory. Perhaps it now feels more like autumn: the harvest has long been reaped, the earth is bare and we fear the coming of a long winter.

Winter has its place in the cycle of the seasons, however. The land and the labourers need rest and time to plan how best to work for future harvests. In these next two weeks, we will look at what lessons we can learn from the church's first 'springtime' to help us work effectively with the Spirit in our own spring season – or wait and plan with hope and faith for when our winter season ends (as it always will, thanks be to our God, Lord of the harvest).

NAOMI STARKEY

The most unlikely apostle

Meanwhile, Saul was still breathing out murderous threats against the Lord's disciples. He went to the high priest and asked him for letters to the synagogues in Damascus, so that if he found any there who belonged to the Way… he might take them as prisoners to Jerusalem. As he neared Damascus… a light from heaven flashed around him. He fell to the ground and heard a voice say to him, 'Saul, Saul, why do you persecute me?' 'Who are you, Lord?' Saul asked. 'I am Jesus, whom you are persecuting,' he replied. 'Now get up and go into the city…' Saul got up from the ground, but when he opened his eyes, he could see nothing.

The opening 'meanwhile' sets us off at the brisk, even breathless, pace that characterises much of Acts. Saul's murderous intentions are at the boil while Philip has been leading the Ethiopian eunuch to faith (8:26–39). What ensues is one of the most astonishing about-turns in scripture. Saul falls to the ground, blinded by the light of the risen Jesus, and he gets up, about to embark on the very 'Way' that he has been dedicated to destroying. He had thought he could see the truth, but his vision needed Christ's transformative touch.

The story is told with Luke's customary flair for dialogue, the repeated 'Saul' emphasising that this is a personal encounter with Jesus rather than a random lightning strike. As Paul (as Saul is renamed) tells it years later to King Agrippa (26:12–18), this is the moment when the Lord commissions him to call the Gentiles from darkness to light and bring them, freed from sin, into God's family.

As we will see, many believers – including the disciples in Jerusalem – were astonished that so fierce an opponent as Saul had experienced such an enormous change. It is a wonderful reminder that nobody is beyond the Lord's reach, something we need to remember today when faith can seem simply an option for those who already like 'that sort of thing'.

Think of somebody you know – either personally or by reputation – who seems for whatever reason 'beyond saving'. Pray that they may encounter the risen Jesus and come into the light of his love.

NAOMI STARKEY

Called to serve and to suffer

In Damascus there was a disciple named Ananias. The Lord called to him in a vision… 'Go to the house of Judas on Straight Street and ask for a man from Tarsus named Saul, for he is praying. In a vision he has seen a man named Ananias come and place his hands on him to restore his sight… This man is my chosen instrument to proclaim my name to the Gentiles and their kings and to the people of Israel. I will show him how much he must suffer for my name.'

This Bible passage is worth reading in full simply for the dramatic dialogue between the Lord and Ananias! Like Moses (Exodus 4:1–13), Ananias at first resists God's call, worrying that he is being given an impossible job (9:13–14). The Holy Spirit has already been at work, though, and (Ananias is told) Saul has received advance notice of his healing and even the name of his healer. God has chosen Ananias for this work, as Saul has also been chosen. All Ananias has to do is obey – and leave the rest to God.

Note the sombre note in the Lord's commission. Saul will be shown 'how much he must suffer'. He has already suffered because of his heavenly encounter, spending his first three days in Damascus sightless, fasting and praying. What lies ahead will be worse. As he later describes (2 Corinthians 11:23–33), he will end up suffering floggings, imprisonment, stoning and shipwreck, as well as the usual rigours of life on the road.

When considering God's call on our lives, what our vocation (to use the jargon) might be, we are more likely to think about how our gifts could best be used and how much personal fulfilment we will gain as a result. We are less likely to ponder the possible hardships involved, let alone anything that could be described as suffering, which we may well equate with 'things going wrong'. In fact, as far as Saul/Paul was concerned, suffering was the expected outcome of his calling, not an accidental by-product.

'Whoever wants to be my disciple must deny themselves and take up their cross daily and follow me' (Luke 9:23).

NAOMI STARKEY

Starting as he means to go on

[Saul] got up and was baptised, and after taking some food, he regained his strength. Saul spent several days with the disciples in Damascus. At once he began to preach in the synagogues that Jesus is the Son of God. All those who heard him were astonished and asked, 'Isn't he the man who caused havoc in Jerusalem among those who call on this name? And hasn't he come here to take them as prisoners to the chief priests?' Yet Saul grew more and more powerful and baffled the Jews living in Damascus by proving that Jesus is the Messiah.

Ananias has been obedient to the Lord's daunting command and come to lay hands on Saul. Doctor Luke notes that 'something like scales fell from Saul's eyes', and then Saul's turnaround is complete as he is baptised. Life has begun again for him; he has been reborn through the Spirit. Starting as he means to go on, he then sets about preaching 'at once', with a message that is a 180-degree reversal of his previous position.

Saul is a well-educated man (22:3) and bursting with energy for whatever cause he espouses. His new direction still proves almost impossible for others to comprehend. As his influence grows, so does the bafflement and astonishment of his audience. This man had not been simply an opposing voice but had been dedicated to physically rooting out Christ's followers. Tomorrow we will hear that he has started to gain his own followers, but we don't know how many; it's hard to gauge the effectiveness of his preaching at this stage.

Those who are bursting with new-found joy in the Lord can be powerful advocates for the gospel; springtime faith is so often wonderfully warming for the autumnal soul. Such enthusiasm, however, still needs tempering with appropriate training and deployment. That can sound drearily jobsworth, but we should remember that the coming of spring in the life of a church will be the Spirit's work; it is not purely dependent on our own efforts.

Father God, may your Holy Spirit be at work in us and in our churches to prepare us for the coming of spring.

NAOMI STARKEY

Turbulent ministry

There was a conspiracy among the Jews to kill [Saul]... But his followers took him by night and lowered him in a basket through an opening
in the wall. When he came to Jerusalem, he tried to join the disciples,
but they were all afraid of him... But Barnabas took him and brought
him to the apostles... Saul stayed with them and moved about freely in
Jerusalem, speaking boldly in the name of the Lord. He talked and
debated with the Hellenistic Jews, but they tried to kill him. When the
believers learned of this, they took him down to Caesarea and sent him
off to Tarsus.

Luke does not say exactly how long Saul ministered in Damascus, but he
does not seem to have enjoyed a honeymoon period of welcome. The
man who was stridently against the Way is now a forthright advocate of it.
Despite (or because of?) his ministerial style, he has gathered followers
about him, who then have to rescue him from his opponents.

Even when he reaches Jerusalem, he is not by any means received with
open arms by the believers there, until Barnabas acts as his advocate.
Barnabas (whom we'll meet again later) is, like Ananias, another in the
supporting cast of the early church. His is not a starring role, but it is an
essential one, a reminder of how the body of Christ can only work effectively if all play their part – as Paul himself was to write later (1 Corinthians
12:12–27).

Saul's work continues to provoke life-threatening opposition – and it's
not impossible that there was relief in the air as the believers waved him
off at Caesarea, homeward-bound. Rapid growth is exciting and headline-
grabbing but also needs careful nurturing to ensure stability. Avoidance of
stress, where possible, generally seems a good idea, but Saul appears to
have a knack for generating stressful situations!

This is far from the end of Saul's part in the story of the early church. It
may have felt like that to him, though, as the Tarsus ship set sail.

Father God, show us how to nurture the growth you send
so that it results in maximum fruitfulness.

NAOMI STARKEY

Growing and flourishing

Then the church throughout Judea, Galilee and Samaria enjoyed a time of peace and was strengthened. Living in the fear of the Lord and encouraged by the Holy Spirit, it increased in numbers. As Peter travelled about the country, he went to visit the Lord's people who lived in Lydda. There he found a man named Aeneas, who was paralysed and had been bedridden for eight years. 'Aeneas,' Peter said to him, 'Jesus Christ heals you. Get up and roll up your mat.' Immediately Aeneas got up. All those who lived in Lydda and Sharon saw him and turned to the Lord.

Following Saul's departure, the young church enjoys a 'time of peace'. It may be that his turbulent ministry still helped to plant seeds that took root and now start to flourish. On the other hand, it may be that peace and growth only happen because he has gone home to Tarsus. What is clear is that the church has become well established beyond Galilee, where Jesus' ministry largely took place. It is even 'throughout' Samaria, that region defined by its otherness, as only close (but unsettlingly different) neighbours can be.

Luke's attention now returns to Peter, last heard of in Samaria, where he sorted out the irregular ministry of Simon the sorcerer (8:9–25). Thriving in his role as the rock upon which the church is founded (Matthew 16:18), Peter is on the road, travelling from one new faith community to another and helping to build up the believers further.

The potential that the Lord himself saw and nurtured in Peter is now being fully realised, in his preaching and Spirit-powered miraculous works. As mentioned in the introduction, these chapters of Acts are full of 'getting up' and 'going out', so it's fitting that the healing of Aeneas is about raising the paralysed man from the bed that has been his prison for eight years, so that he too can 'get up' – and do so 'immediately'!

Who might be a 'Peter' in our local church, one whose gifts need nurturing so that they can serve God's purposes, as God has always intended them to do?

NAOMI STARKEY

Given back for now

In Joppa there was a disciple named Tabitha (in Greek her name is Dorcas); she was always doing good and helping the poor. About that time she became ill and died, and her body was washed and placed in an upstairs room... When [Peter] arrived he was taken upstairs to the room. All the widows stood round him, crying and showing him the robes and other clothing that Dorcas had made... Peter sent them all out of the room; then he got down on his knees and prayed. Turning towards the dead woman, he said, 'Tabitha, get up.' She opened her eyes, and seeing Peter she sat up.

Peter has been summoned from Lydda to the port of Joppa (Jaffa), home of Tabitha/Dorcas. Working as I do in the bilingual (English/Welsh) diocese of Bangor, it's fascinating to be reminded that the church first took root in a bilingual or even multilingual context.

We're not given much detail about Tabitha herself, but we hear how dear she was to others. Hers was not cold charity but energetic love in action. In today's world of cheap fashion, we can overlook the effort and generosity involved in clothing those in need back then. The widows' tears at her passing were mingled with pride, as they showed Peter the garments that Tabitha had given them. They may well have begged him, 'Don't let her leave us! Do whatever you can to bring her back – please.' And Peter hears them, prays and lifts Tabitha, alive again, to her feet.

Stories are still shared of the dead being raised in some parts of the world, but we should not impute the lack of such miracles in our own experience to lack of faith – or lack of good deeds by the one who has died. Tabitha came back (and one day would die again) and many more did not, who believed and served God just as faithfully, yet whose stories are not recorded in scripture.

Give thanks for those you've known whose good deeds and kind hearts have touched your life. Commend to God's care, too, those whose names are known only to him, whose deeds and kindnesses are now forgotten by all except their Father in heaven.

NAOMI STARKEY

The Spirit is moving

At Caesarea there was a man named Cornelius, a centurion in what was known as the Italian Regiment. He and all his family were devout and God-fearing; he gave generously to those in need and prayed to God regularly. One day at about three in the afternoon he had a vision. He distinctly saw an angel of God, who came to him and said, 'Cornelius!… Your prayers and gifts to the poor have come up as a memorial offering before God. Now send men to Joppa to bring back a man named Simon who is called Peter. He is staying with Simon the tanner, whose house is by the sea.'

Peter has been staying at the house of Simon, a local tanner, as the news of Tabitha's miraculous return to life spreads around Joppa (9:42–43). Now the scene shifts abruptly to a wider and different world: the Roman empire, represented by the figure of Cornelius, a 'devout and God-fearing' centurion.

Cornelius has not been affected by the Tabitha episode; he has his own theophany, a vision of God's messenger addressing him as directly and clearly as that which happened to Ananias. Even though he is not told why he should invite Peter over, Cornelius is quick to obey (10:7–8). His disciplined life of prayer and good works has prepared his heart for such an experience.

We may long for springtime growth, but such growth calls for the hard work of preparation: pruning the dead wood, tilling the soil, sowing the seed. Cornelius was on a journey with God before his vision; his angelic encounter leads him further along a path to which he is already committed.

What unfolds from Cornelius' vision will prove seismic for the young church, pushing the believers beyond familiar securities and also paving the way for Saul/Paul's ministry to the Gentile world.

Note how Cornelius 'gave generously to those in need' as well as praying regularly. In our own church life today, practical involvement can prove an open door into knowing God for many, even before they have taken a formal step of faith.

NAOMI STARKEY

Dirty made clean

Peter went up on the roof to pray. He became hungry and wanted something to eat, and while the meal was being prepared he fell into a trance. He saw heaven opened and something like a large sheet being let down to earth by its four corners. It contained all kinds of four-footed animals, as well as reptiles and birds. Then a voice told him, 'Get up, Peter. Kill and eat.' 'Surely not, Lord!' Peter replied. 'I have never eaten anything impure or unclean.' The voice spoke to him a second time, 'Do not call anything impure that God has made clean.'

The scene shifts again as the drama builds. Cornelius has sent two servants and a 'devout soldier' to fetch Peter. We see them approaching the city in the noonday sun and then the focus narrows to a man on a flat roof. Peter has sought out a quiet place to pray (like his Lord did) and is now waiting for his lunch. Then he too has a vision. Was it a food-based vision because he was hungry? Possibly – but whatever the cause, the outcome is shocking in the extreme. God himself tells Peter that he can break one of the central tenets of his God-given faith and eat ritually unclean food.

For most of us, it's hard to feel the full force of Peter's shock. This isn't just a matter of eating dirty food, such as other people's leftovers or sharing the dog's dish. The rules about clean and unclean food were part of Peter's identity, part of that which made him and his family different from people like Cornelius, from the Gentile world as a whole.

What the vision seems to say, however, is that God made the rules, so God can change the rules. In the same way, Jesus spoke of the sabbath being 'made for man, not man for the Sabbath' (Mark 2:27) and sat down to dine with people others deemed undesirable – the morally wayward, the collaborators and so on.

Do you have a line in the sand, an issue that you feel definitively marks someone out as a Christ-follower or unbeliever? How would you feel if you heard God say, 'I have made this, too, clean'?

NAOMI STARKEY

A question of timing

While Peter was still thinking about the vision, the Spirit said to him, 'Simon, three men are looking for you. So get up and go downstairs. Do not hesitate to go with them, for I have sent them'… The next day Peter started out with them, and some of the believers from Joppa went along. The following day he arrived in Caesarea. Cornelius was expecting them and had called together his relatives and close friends. As Peter entered the house, Cornelius met him and fell at his feet in reverence. But Peter made him get up. 'Stand up,' he said, 'I am only a man myself.'

Helpfully, the Spirit's direction to Peter is clear and unequivocal, as it had been to Cornelius. Sometimes people describe their experience of guidance in similar terms: 'So I said to God… and then God said to me…' – as if it were a chat over coffee with a friend. In fact, like so many matters of faith, guidance can appear straightforward yet turn out to be complex in practice.

We should view Peter's openness to the Spirit within the context of his disciplines of prayer and listening to God, as well as the years already spent as a disciple. The energetic, impatient man has learnt to reflect and wait, lessons that perhaps Saul has been painfully acquiring, back home in Tarsus, lessons essential for all in leadership.

Having heard the Spirit's prompt, Peter is ready to receive his unexpected visitors, and the next day they set off for Caesarea. It's worth thinking about how long this took. Caesarea was nearly a day's journey from Joppa, so Cornelius' men had a sleepover with Peter before their return. We're told the party arrived 'the following day', suggesting that the trip took longer this time. I wonder what conversations took place during those hours together on the road, as well as the evening in Joppa. Perhaps by the time Peter arrived, he was in the company of friends.

Peter describes himself as 'only a man'. Pray for those in authority in your local church (including yourself, if appropriate), that they may remember that they too are only human, working under the Spirit's direction.

NAOMI STARKEY

Good news for everyone

Then Peter began to speak: 'I now realise how true it is that God does not show favouritism but accepts from every nation the one who fears him and does what is right… You know what has happened throughout the province of Judea, beginning in Galilee after the baptism that John preached – how God anointed Jesus of Nazareth with the Holy Spirit and power, and how he went around doing good and healing all who were under the power of the devil, because God was with him… All the prophets testify about him that everyone who believes in him receives forgiveness of sins through his name.'

Following Peter's arrival, Cornelius rehearses his story and explains why he has summoned the apostle. Faced with a 'large gathering' (v. 27) in this Gentile household, Peter may well have taken a deep breath before responding. It's interesting to note that he assumes familiarity with the story of 'Jesus of Nazareth'; his audience will apparently have heard about what happened, but now Peter can interpret and connect the events with their own lives. He can explain to them that through Jesus' death and resurrection, all who believe can receive forgiveness.

Peter admits that the very fact of his presence in that household is a huge step for him, and the necessary shift in mindset remained a stumbling block for the early church for years to come (as demonstrated, for example, by the letter to the Galatians). Such a shift is, however, the fulfilment of Jesus' command to his disciples: 'Go and make disciples of all nations' (Matthew 28:19). It is a fulfilment, too, of the prophetic vision found throughout scripture of the nations coming to worship at the throne of God. The salvation won on the cross is for everyone, without qualification.

'I did not see a temple in the city, because the Lord God Almighty and the Lamb are its temple. The city does not need the sun or the moon to shine on it, for the glory of God gives it light, and the Lamb is its lamp. The nations will walk by its light, and the kings of the earth will bring their splendour into it' (Revelation 21:22–24).

NAOMI STARKEY

Break through

While Peter was still speaking these words, the Holy Spirit came on all who heard the message. The circumcised believers who had come with Peter were astonished that the gift of the Holy Spirit had been poured out even on Gentiles. For they heard them speaking in tongues and praising God. Then Peter said, 'Surely no one can stand in the way of their being baptised with water. They have received the Holy Spirit just as we have.' So he ordered that they be baptised in the name of Jesus Christ. Then they asked Peter to stay with them for a few days.

Peter hasn't even finished his address. He hasn't given any kind of altar call nor given any suggestion as to what his hearers should do next (apart from 'believe'). Without waiting even for baptism, the Holy Spirit falls upon these people who, as 'God-fearers', could be considered, in faith terms, cousins rather than brothers and sisters. Thus, new life bursts out in Caesarea, with praise and heavenly worship baffling and then delighting the visitors.

In travelling to Cornelius' house, Peter had literally come more than halfway towards the enquirers, while in his preaching he had started with what they already knew (the story of Jesus of Nazareth). There's a pattern for us to follow here, as we seek to engage with those who approach the local church wanting a wedding, a baptism or a funeral. They may or may not know much of faith, but they want to connect, if only briefly, with what the church represents. Who knows how the Spirit may have been at work in their lives – or what will happen in the future, if like Peter we come more than halfway to meet them?

Open to the Spirit's guidance, Peter accepts the new believers' invitation to stay for a few days. Nurturing relationship is, once again, shown to be a key part of ministry. That's a challenge for leaders today, so often constrained by busy schedules from simply hanging around to see what God might do next.

Lord God, show us how to find the right balance between careful plans and strategies – and keeping hearts open to your Spirit's call.

NAOMI STARKEY

Stepping outside the comfort zone

The apostles and the believers throughout Judea heard that the Gentiles also had received the word of God. So when Peter went up to Jerusalem, the circumcised believers criticised him and said, 'You went into the house of uncircumcised men and ate with them.' Starting from the beginning, Peter told them the whole story... 'If God gave them the same gift he gave us who believed in the Lord Jesus Christ, who was I to think that I could stand in God's way?' When they heard this, they had no further objections and praised God, saying, 'So then, even to Gentiles God has granted repentance that leads to life.'

The joyous outcome at Cornelius' house proves a bump in the road to the church's Jerusalem HQ, another reminder that Peter's actions were not just unprecedented but shocking. Far from being angrily defensive, though, Peter tells his story, this time referring to what Jesus had told them: baptism in the Spirit was a development of John's baptism in water (11:16). This means, Peter reflects, that God was at work in Caesarea – and who can 'stand in God's way'?

After receiving this considered response to their criticism, the objections of the 'circumcised believers' turn to praise. They are willing to step out of their comfort zone and submit themselves to the God who is just as likely to move despite tidy rules and structures as he is because of them. What they had thought of as 'their' faith is proving to be something intended to bless the world, not indirectly through their efforts but in direct transformation.

Paul would later write: 'There is neither Jew nor Gentile, neither slave nor free, nor is there male and female, for you are all one in Christ Jesus. If you belong to Christ, then you are Abraham's seed, and heirs according to the promise' (Galatians 3:28–29). That truth has proved astonishingly hard to hold on to, as church history has shown. It appears that little delights the human heart more than deciding who is 'in' and who is 'out'.

---

*Maybe God's actions are sometimes chaotic, messy, even 'dirty'
by our usual standards.*

NAOMI STARKEY

Further afield

Now those who had been scattered by the persecution that broke out when Stephen was killed travelled as far as Phoenicia, Cyprus and Antioch, spreading the word only among Jews. Some of them, however, men from Cyprus and Cyrene, went to Antioch and began to speak to Greeks also... The Lord's hand was with them, and a great number of people believed... News of this reached the church in Jerusalem, and they sent Barnabas to Antioch. When he arrived and saw what the grace of God had done, he was glad and encouraged them all to remain true to the Lord with all their hearts.

As has happened throughout history, the gospel spreads as people move about, whether because of trade, migration or (as here) persecution. Out of apparent disaster, God is bringing good (see Romans 8:28). Now, out of Peter's courageous obedience to the Spirit's command, the good news is carried beyond Jewish communities to their Greek neighbours. Jerusalem continues its supervisory role, keeping a careful eye on developments and dispatching our old friend Barnabas to check that all is well in Antioch.

At one time the third-largest city in the empire (after Rome and Alexandria), Antioch was in Asia Minor (present-day Turkey), not to be confused with Antioch in Pisidia, which Barnabas later visited with Paul (13:14–51). Numerous Orthodox and eastern Catholic churches trace their history back to the church founded there in the first century – a reminder of Christianity's roots as an eastern faith.

Barnabas' mission shows us that growth, especially vigorous spring-time growth, needs careful tending. It's not a matter of control but of training, so that energy is channelled in the right directions and results in good fruit, which will be evidence of the Holy Spirit's working, as Paul would tell the Galatians (5:22–23). Finding signs of God's grace in the new faith community's life, Barnabas can affirm them and encourage them to persevere on the Way.

Think about your local community. Are there 'incomers' who have brought new energy to the churches? Thank God for them and reflect on how to make them feel as welcomed as possible.

NAOMI STARKEY

A good man

[Barnabas] was a good man, full of the Holy Spirit and faith… [He] went to Tarsus to look for Saul, and when he found him, he brought him to Antioch. So for a whole year Barnabas and Saul met with the church and taught great numbers of people. The disciples were called Christians first at Antioch. During this time some prophets came down from Jerusalem to Antioch. One of them… through the Spirit predicted that a severe famine would spread over the entire Roman world… The disciples, as each one was able, decided to provide help for the brothers and sisters living in Judea.

The church in Antioch continues its springtime flourishing, and its role as a new centre of the faith is underlined by others arriving to share in the ministry. Wonderfully, the believers are then able to send aid to their brothers and sisters in Christ back in Judea. Perhaps this generous act was in part inspired by their mentor Barnabas, who is characterised by generosity from his first appearance (4:36–37), when he sells a field and gives the money to the apostles.

As well as generous, Barnabas is portrayed as instinctively encouraging. His birth name was Joseph, but the apostles give him the name Barnabas, which, Luke says, means 'son of encouragement' (a bit like Simon becoming 'Peter/Rock' in Matthew 16:18). Antioch could have been Barnabas' opportunity to build 'his' church, but instead he goes in search of Saul so that together they disciple the church. Their partnership only comes to an end when they disagree over offering a junior colleague a second chance (15:37–39). Typically, Barnabas wants to do so.

Mentoring those younger in the faith is a priceless gift. So many church leaders can point to someone who took an interest in them at an early stage, giving them opportunities to have a go and make mistakes and encouraging them. Without such people, generous in patience and time, forgiving but also offering inspiration, the church would be immensely impoverished.

Lord God, send more people like Barnabas to our churches –
and show me how I can be a Barnabas too.

NAOMI STARKEY

Proverbs

I have recently become a prison chaplain. The work is very interesting but very demanding – every day brings new challenges. As part of my role, I hold regular Bible studies in the prison, accompanying residents as they look at the scriptures and reflect on what has happened in their lives that has led them to jail. Proverbs is the perfect book for me to use because it is a reflection on experience rather than straight teaching or commands. It can be used to introduce the Bible to those who are new to the faith and want to learn the ways of God in the world.

Proverbs is an anthology of sayings, so it is best digested a few at a time. The depth of its language means that it needs to be absorbed slowly. If you read your way carefully, reflectively and lovingly through the book, you will learn the wisdom of God for daily life. It is important to note that the proverbs are generalisations, rather than invariably true. For example, proverbs which claim that those who live by God's standards will prosper (e.g. 16:20) are not giving an unqualified promise to all believers, as is shown by the stories of the many Old Testament characters, such as Job, Joseph and Moses, who underwent hardships and setbacks. The lives of Christ and his followers also show us that pain and suffering are to be expected in this world.

In content, the book of Proverbs belongs to the days of Israel's first kings, though editing continued for some centuries. King Solomon's name appears in the title, and he is the author and compiler of the two longest collections (10:1—22:16). King Hezekiah, who organised some of the editorial work (25:1), reigned 250 years after Solomon. Solomon was a wise man (1 Kings 4:30). He built the temple so that the ark of the covenant could be housed and the Israelites could worship the Lord. He started on the book of Proverbs so that his people might live out God's teaching. Across the generations ever since, the book of Proverbs has been helping people to live out God's plan for their lives.

BOB MAYO

Wise living

The proverbs of Solomon son of David, king of Israel: for gaining wisdom and instruction; for understanding words of insight; for receiving instruction in prudent behaviour, doing what is right and just and fair; for giving prudence to those who are simple, knowledge and discretion to the young – let the wise listen and add to their learning, and let the discerning get guidance – for understanding proverbs and parables, the sayings and riddles of the wise. The fear of the Lord is the beginning of knowledge, but fools despise wisdom and instruction.

The penultimate phrase from this passage – 'the fear of the Lord is the beginning of knowledge' – lies at the heart of Proverbs. This is 'fear' in the sense of reverence and awe rather than terror. Jesus has called us his friends (John 15:15) and we don't go about in terror of our friends.

This is 'fear' acted out through disciplined behaviour rather than simply experienced as a feeling. In our society it is easy to think of our faith in terms of how it makes us feel: if I pray, I want to feel at peace; if I sing, I want to feel uplifted. Proverbs teaches us that a life of faith is a decision and a lifestyle. It is our choice to follow God's commands. A fear of the Lord doesn't come about because of what we feel; it comes because of what we do as a result of what we feel. When Isaiah sees the majesty of God in the temple, he cries out, 'Here am I. Send me!' (Isaiah 6:8). He has seen God's majesty and he wants to respond.

The book of Proverbs says that a wise life is lived in response to the mystery of God's love. The first question that wisdom asks is: how do you choose to spend your time? Prayer is a good place to start. The Bible asks you to pray both alone (Matthew 6:5–6) and in church with other believers (Hebrews 10:25).

Lord, help me to spend my time wisely – and let me begin with prayer.

BOB MAYO

'Do not forget my teaching'

My son, do not forget my teaching, but keep my commands in your heart, for they will prolong your life many years and bring you peace and prosperity. Let love and faithfulness never leave you; bind them round your neck, write them on the tablet of your heart. Then you will win favour and a good name in the sight of God and man. Trust in the Lord with all your heart and lean not on your own understanding; in all your ways submit to him, and he will make your paths straight. Do not be wise in your own eyes; fear the Lord and shun evil.

Children learn about the faith more at home with their parents than at church with Sunday school. According to Proverbs, it is the task of family members more than the church to 'start children off on the way they should go, and even when they are old they will not turn from it' (22:6). There can be a temptation for parents to think of going to church with their children as being like dropping the children off at school: with the kids out of the way at Sunday school, they have a right to enjoy their adult worship. Proverbs makes it clear that this should not be so.

However, this is not to say that what happens at church for children is unimportant. Christian communities have a vital role in providing support, encouragement and teaching for those who are helping to raise the next generation. This can take place not only in the structured environment of Sunday teaching, but also in the attitude of older members of the community towards the younger ones – welcoming and encouraging – and in the support that is offered to all those who work with and for children and young people. Even worshipping communities without children can support their local school or community centre with voluntary help or funding for books, demonstrating their faith through the practical action of their lives.

How can you help and encourage children in your church community?

BOB MAYO

117

Don't be lazy

Go to the ant, you sluggard; consider its ways and be wise! It has no commander, no overseer or ruler, yet it stores its provisions in summer and gathers its food at harvest. How long will you lie there, you sluggard? When will you get up from your sleep? A little sleep, a little slumber, a little folding of the hands to rest – and poverty will come on you like a thief and scarcity like an armed man.

Work and laziness are recurring themes in Proverbs. Laziness (sloth) is one of the seven deadly sins. This is something different to unemployment. In our society, with an ageing population and increasing life expectancy, people can be many years retired from paid employment. Retirement has now become akin to changing the tyres on the car before setting off on a new journey of travel, study or voluntary work for the good of the wider community. In a digital age, work can mean full- or part-time self-employment. It is also not unusual for people to take a career break, and unemployment for some people can continue for many years.

What this passage condemns is laziness. Just as God condemns wicked things, such as murder, adultery and lying, so also does he condemn laziness (Matthew 25:26). Residents at the prison where I work are relearning their place in society. They have a saying, 'You arrive on your own and you leave on your own'; in other words, each person must take responsibility for their own actions. They are having to learn to do what the Bible teaches us all to do. Timothy warns that people who don't have enough to do can become gossips, slanderers and busybodies (1 Timothy 5:13–14).

Someone can be in full-time employment, yet become lazy if they take people for granted, don't learn people's names and cut corners when it comes to getting a job done. A person can be unemployed and yet work hard if they use their time meaningfully, for example, by caring for the vulnerable and poor in the community.

Are there ways in which you are lazy? How might you avoid this?

BOB MAYO

Church – not just Sundays

The Lord detests dishonest scales, but accurate weights find favour with him. When pride comes, then comes disgrace, but with humility comes wisdom. The integrity of the upright guides them, but the unfaithful are destroyed by their duplicity. Wealth is worthless in the day of wrath, but righteousness delivers from death. The righteousness of the blameless makes their paths straight, but the wicked are brought down by their own wickedness. The righteousness of the upright delivers them, but the unfaithful are trapped by evil desires.

One of the criticisms of contemporary churchgoing is that what happens on Sunday in church has very little to do with everyday life, and this is particularly the case with our working lives. It is easy to think of business practice and belief in God as being in two separate categories, but the God of heaven and earth approves of good business practice, just as he approves of any good practice. The message repeated throughout Proverbs is that if you are wise you will recognise that God is not only Lord of your heart but is also in charge of your day-to-day decision-making. The hymns that you sing, the sermons that you listen to and the conversations that you have at church on Sunday have to be acted on throughout the week.

With wisdom comes humility, integrity and righteousness. The origin of the word 'humility' is the Latin word *humus*, meaning fertile ground. *Humus* helps plants to thrive, and humble people do likewise, bringing out the best in others. The origin of the word 'integrity' is the Latin word *integer*, meaning wholeness or completeness. Integrity is about doing the right thing (being righteous) even when it's not acknowledged by others.

With pride comes deceit, dishonour and disgrace. There are times in the prison when residents want to turn their back on their previous pride-filled lifestyle and commit themselves to a new life in Christ. One resident said that, although he was shut behind locked doors, he had never felt more free since he became a Christian.

Lord, let me praise you 'seven whole days, not one in seven'
(George Herbert, 1633).

BOB MAYO

Justice is not an optional extra

Whoever oppresses the poor shows contempt for their Maker, but whoever is kind to the needy honours God... Evildoers do not understand what is right, but those who seek the Lord understand it fully... Speak up for those who cannot speak for themselves, for the rights of all who are destitute. Speak up and judge fairly; defend the rights of the poor and needy.

A concern for the poor and dispossessed is woven into the fabric of the Old Testament. At the heart of Israel's national identity was a history of slavery. Each year the people were to celebrate the Passover, remembering that they were slaves in the land of Egypt and were redeemed by God (Deuteronomy 15:15). The Israelites were thus commanded to look after the poor in their community. At harvest time, for example, they were not to reap to the very edges of their fields or gather the gleanings of the harvest; these were to be left for the poor (Leviticus 23:22). In an agricultural society people are not set up in competition with each other, but work together cooperatively to harvest the land.

God's heart for the poor, marginalised, vulnerable and oppressed is almost shocking in its obviousness. There are few things more present, more apparent throughout the Bible. In our world, justice needs to be thought of in global terms. The price we pay for commodities may affect the wages paid in developing countries. Cheap labour costs may come as a result of human trafficking.

Homelessness and loneliness are two significant issues in our society. In the prison where I work, the residents have to face up to issues of justice as they come to terms with their situation. In our Good Friday service, one resident opened his testimony dramatically: 'Jesus was banged up and was innocent; we are banged up and are guilty.' The wisdom of God is liberating and life-giving, not only for the individual but also for their wider society.

How can we ensure that justice is not seen as an optional extra to our Christian life and that a concern for the poor is seen as the responsibility of everyone?

BOB MAYO

Tongue control!

A gentle answer turns away wrath, but a harsh word stirs up anger. The tongue of the wise adorns knowledge, but the mouth of the fool gushes folly… From the fruit of their mouth a person's stomach is filled; with the harvest of their lips they are satisfied. The tongue has the power of life and death, and those who love it will eat its fruit.

There are few things more destructive to communities than gossip and spite, few things more fundamental in building a community of faith than guarding what we say and how we say it. The wisdom of this passage is repeated throughout the Old Testament and is emphasised in the New Testament. Jesus asserts that a person is not defiled by what goes into their mouth but by what comes out of it (Matthew 15:11). James 3:8–10 says, 'No human being can tame the tongue. It is a restless evil, full of deadly poison. With the tongue we praise our Lord and Father, and with it we curse human beings, who have been made in God's likeness. Out of the same mouth come praise and cursing.'

You are being ill-disciplined in the use of your tongue if you feel that it is important for you always to have the last word in a conversation. It means that you are probably not fully concentrating on what the other person is saying because you are preoccupied with what you would like to say next. You do violence to people with words when you talk behind their backs. Francis of Assisi said it was better to maintain a silence than to speak ill of another.

In conversations if you tell yourself that you are being 'honest', it may in reality mean simply that you are being critical. In a digital world it is easy for us not to see the consequences of our words and the extent to which our words can help to make people feel better or worse about themselves.

How can you use words for the good of others? If one person speaks positively about another, maybe you are in a position to pass on the details of that conversation to the other person.

BOB MAYO

Anybody can be wise

Mockers resent correction, so they avoid the wise. A happy heart makes the face cheerful, but heartache crushes the spirit. The discerning heart seeks knowledge, but the mouth of a fool feeds on folly. All the days of the oppressed are wretched, but the cheerful heart has a continual feast. Better a little with the fear of the Lord than great wealth with turmoil. Better a dish of vegetables with love than a fattened calf with hatred. A hot-tempered person stirs up conflict, but the one who is patient calms a quarrel. The way of the sluggard is blocked with thorns, but the path of the upright is a highway.

The good news is that anyone can be wise. Wisdom is not like an examination that you pass or fail. It is a process of continual learning and growth: if you want to learn, you grow, and if you want to grow, you learn. In this passage there is no halfway house: to stop learning is 'folly'; to carry on learning is 'discerning'.

Wise people never stop learning. One of the easiest ways to keep learning is to look and to listen to people talk. There are increased levels of loneliness in our society, and people are glad to have someone to talk to who is willing to listen to them. Loneliness is not restricted to old age: according to a BBC survey in 2018, 18–24-year-olds are the loneliest age group.

The good news of Proverbs is that God's teaching works in practice, and wisdom marks herself with well-lived lives. Wise people are discerning, loving and cheerful. They want the best for other people, so they try to be patient and calm any quarrels. Wise people have their priorities straight, valuing love more than material wealth (which is the point of verse 17, rather than a comment on vegetarianism over meat-eating). It is no surprise that their path is a highway, while the way of the sluggard is blocked with thorns.

Wisdom is not just for holy people: if you seek wisdom, you will find her (Proverbs 2:3–5).

BOB MAYO

We choose our attitude

Above all else, guard your heart, for everything you do flows from it. Keep your mouth free of perversity; keep corrupt talk far from your lips. Let your eyes look straight ahead; fix your gaze directly before you. Give careful thought to the paths for your feet and be steadfast in all your ways. Do not turn to the right or the left; keep your foot from evil.

Here we learn that wisdom does not come with big plans, clever ideas or impressive ambitions. Wisdom starts quietly with careful thoughts, straight talk and a steadfast, reliable character. Wisdom is not distracted by what might appear to be more attractive options. A wise person is someone people trust, because you know where you stand with them.

A wise person is not easily distracted and understands that the attitude they adopt in a situation is a matter of choice. Often our situations come about because of the choices we have made; at other times, circumstances beyond our control may dictate our situation. The one thing we can control is our attitude towards what has happened.

In my work in the prison, I meet with some residents whose lives have been strangled by bitterness and disappointed expectations. I meet others with a wise attitude – they guard their heart and keep their eyes looking straight ahead. Some are crushed by a sense of injustice at what has happened to them, while others are determined to make the best of the situation.

One resident recently told me that he read the Bible, cover to cover, in seven weeks – one thing of which there is no shortage in prison is time! He said that he began to feel free in prison once he discovered that Paul did his best work while in a similar situation. Another resident said to me that coming to prison was the best thing that ever happened to him, because it gave him time to learn a skill and to get himself in order.

Lord, help me to be loving and resolute, firm and forward-looking in all I think and do.

BOB MAYO

Be a friend to get a friend

A scoundrel plots evil, and on their lips it is like a scorching fire. A perverse person stirs up conflict, and a gossip separates close friends… A friend loves at all times, and a brother is born for a time of adversity… The purposes of a person's heart are deep waters, but one who has insight draws them out… Whoever conceals their sins does not prosper, but the one who confesses and renounces them finds mercy.

One of Proverbs' many themes is friendship. Friendship is not simply commanded or commended as a way of life; its fundamental importance is indicated in the way that instructions are given on how to be a good friend. To be a good friend you have to be discreet and not stir up trouble. You have to be dependable when things are difficult. You have to give your heart to the relationship and not be superficial. You have to be honest about your sins and not try to hide them.

According to Proverbs, friendships don't simply happen; they need work and application. Learning how to be a friend to others is a good skill for modern-day living, because it involves making relationships where other connections might have been lost – families may have moved away and people left isolated and alone. For some, friendships will be made online; for others, friendship-making will be with people in the local community. It is easy to assume that everyone else has plenty of friends, whereas they may be glad for some contact from you. Sometimes at church people can leave a Sunday service not having talked with anyone.

Friendships are the opposite of taking people for granted. Friendship-making is important, because it means thinking beyond yourself. C.S. Lewis wrote that 'lovers are normally face-to-face, absorbed in each other; friends are side by side, absorbed in some common interest' (*The Four Loves*, 1960). Jesus said, 'I no longer call you servants, because a servant does not know his master's business. Instead, I have called you friends, for everything that I learned from my Father I have made known to you' (John 15:15).

Dear Lord, help me to be a friend to others
and to think of them before myself.

BOB MAYO

Disagreeing well

For he guards the course of the just and protects the way of his faithful ones. Then you will understand what is right and just and fair – every good path. For wisdom will enter your heart, and knowledge will be pleasant to your soul. Discretion will protect you, and understanding will guard you… As iron sharpens iron, so one person sharpens another.

The book of Proverbs doesn't just explore close relationships, such as family and friends. It also shares wisdom with us about how to get along with those people with whom we might not naturally agree, because it is from these people that we often have the most to learn. In today's church, people often use the word 'spirituality' rather than wisdom. This can be dangerous, as spirituality can be thought of as a term for the individual, reflecting the isolationism and egotism of contemporary society. Individualism can lead to isolation and isolation to loneliness; relationships can bring well-being and fullness of life.

It is natural to spend time with those with whom we feel comfortable. When meeting together for worship and fellowship, we tend to gravitate towards those people we like. Our friends on Facebook or our followers on Twitter are likely to be those who agree with our point of view. The wisdom of Proverbs crosses the boundaries of relationships that we set ourselves, declaring that 'as iron sharpens iron, so one person sharpens another', helping us to learn and grow from points of conflict.

A person who is wise knows the art of learning from others, disagreeing well and not being defensive. The art of disagreeing well is often especially needed at family gatherings. It is an art we wish many of our politicians could learn. In prison, people are rethinking how to live their lives and I gain insights from their observations. One resident said to me, 'I am probably learning more than you at the moment because you are busier than me.' Another said, of the time sat in his cell: 'They can lock the lock, but they can't stop the clock.'

Dear God, help me to learn from others without growing defensive.

BOB MAYO

Lord of our money

How much better to get wisdom than gold, to get insight rather than silver! The highway of the upright avoids evil; those who guard their ways preserve their lives. Pride goes before destruction, a haughty spirit before a fall. Better to be lowly in spirit along with the oppressed than to share plunder with the proud. Whoever gives heed to instruction prospers, and blessed is the one who trusts in the Lord. The wise in heart are called discerning, and gracious words promote instruction.

The pressure in our society to think of money is immense. What about the debt I will get from going to university? What if I lose my job? Do I have enough money for my pension? We learn in this passage that if we first fix our hearts on gaining wisdom and insight, then we will discover that however much gold and silver we obtain will be sufficient for us. If, however, we put making money first on our list of priorities, we will never be satisfied and our wisdom will not increase.

It takes wisdom for a parent to teach a child that material possessions do not indicate moral wealth. It takes wisdom for a student on limited funds to resist the call to an expensive night out just to fit in with their fellow students. It takes wisdom for us to judge others on how they behave rather than how much money they have.

Trust in God runs down the central spine of all the teaching in Proverbs and is at the heart of a life lived wisely. In prison, I meet with people who have put their trust in gold rather than God, which has brought them no reward. Prison is a period of incarceration, when residents rethink how they want to live their lives. One person who is determined to live his life differently said to me, 'I will keep my head down and my chin up' (mind my own business and be resolute), and 'Borrowing is double bubble' (don't get into debt).

Lord, help me to put my trust in you when it comes to financial decisions of the mind as well as relationship decisions of the heart.

BOB MAYO

Too many choices

Trust in the Lord with all your heart and lean not on your own understanding; in all your ways submit to him, and he will make your paths straight… Anxiety weighs down the heart, but a kind word cheers it up… The one who guards a fig-tree will eat its fruit, and whoever protects their master will be honoured. As water reflects the face, so one's life reflects the heart.

Working in a prison, I am with people at the turning of their worlds, rethinking their place in society. The residents learn to give up what they can't control, as they become subject to the rules and regulations of the institution. Those who accept this with good grace are those who have begun the process of rebuilding their lives. 'Don't worry,' one resident said to me, 'about what you can't see on the other side of the wall.'

We, as Christians, are also asked to give up control of our lives – not to a prison system, but instead to a loving God in whom we can confidently place our trust. Once we place our trust in the Lord, life becomes more straightforward. We are no longer anxious, and our paths are made straight. We will eat the fruit of the fig tree, and we will be honoured for protecting the name of the Lord. Anxiety is worrying needlessly about those multiple daily decisions in life that can drain us of our energy. Trust is giving over control of our lives to God.

In our society we are battered by choices about what to do with our time. It is easy to be anxious because we feel that we are missing out. Social media causes anxiety to many people because they are comparing themselves to someone else's apparently perfect life. Jesus tells us not to worry (Matthew 6:25), to take one day at a time (Matthew 6:34) and to let our 'yes' be 'yes' and our 'no' be 'no' (Matthew 5:37). It is a wise way to live.

Lord, keep me free from anxiety and help me to put my trust in you.

BOB MAYO

The third age

The wise in heart are called discerning, and gracious words promote instruction. Prudence is a fountain of life to the prudent, but folly brings punishment to fools. The hearts of the wise make their mouths prudent, and their lips promote instruction. Gracious words are a honeycomb, sweet to the soul and healing to the bones… Grey hair is a crown of splendour; it is attained in the way of righteousness. Better a patient person than a warrior, one with self-control than one who takes a city. The lot is cast into the lap, but its every decision is from the Lord.

Wise living eventually becomes a part of who we are rather than simply a question of making right and wrong choices. Wisdom repays those who seek her face (4:8) and she becomes an integral part of our character. Wise people are discerning and gracious, prudent and patient. In the New Testament we are told to pray for these qualities; they are the fruit of the Spirit (Galatians 5:22–23).

In our society, these are the qualities often shown by the silver-haired generation, who have had time to reflect on a lifetime of experience. Church communities are often dismayed at the average age of their congregations – this should not be so. Provided that safeguarding proce-dures are properly in place and followed scrupulously, one of the most valuable things that the church has to offer to young people is simple, uncomplicated relationships with adults. One of the young people in the prison wanted a Bible because it reminded him of times he had spent with his grandmother. One of the best youth workers I have known was a silver-haired lady in her 80s. She had time to listen to the young people telling her their stories. The church is making a mistake if, by focusing its mission energy on young people, it doesn't give respect to the contributions able to be made to church life by older people.

Lord, help me to be proud of the value that older people
bring to our church community.

BOB MAYO

God knows best

In the Lord's hand the king's heart is a stream of water that he channels towards all who please him. A person may think their own ways are right, but the Lord weighs the heart. To do what is right and just is more acceptable to the Lord than sacrifice… There is no wisdom, no insight, no plan that can succeed against the Lord. The horse is made ready for the day of battle, but victory rests with the Lord.

I work with people whose lives have been broken, and I am offering them no real or substantial hope if I tell them that the world is random or arbitrary. Thankfully, Christ has overcome the world, and I can encourage residents at the prison to rejoin a society that is part of a world of meaning and purpose, underpinned and guided by the love of God. Ultimately, true wisdom belongs to God and our own wisdom can only reflect this. God tells Jeremiah (1:5) that he knew him before he was even formed in the womb. Proverbs teaches us to equip ourselves for wise living, and ultimately the wisest thing of all is to rest in the Lord and to recognise that God will direct our hearts and use our plans to his glory.

The proverbs in today's reading should not be read as a confrontational relationship between God and human beings, as if we are going to battle against each other. They say that God channels the heart like a stream of water; God weighs the heart; to do what is right and just is more acceptable than sacrifice. God brings his purpose and makes his plans out of all that we do. There is nothing that we can do to thwart this. This is a comforting thought for the residents at the prison, who have so much to do to rebuild their lives. It is a hopeful thought for all of us conscious of the sin in our lives and the need to fix our eyes on Jesus, the pioneer and perfecter of faith (Hebrews 12:2).

Lord, help me to put my trust in you always.
I can only do my best and leave you to do the rest. Amen

BOB MAYO

Songs of praise

I really enjoy the BBC Radio 4 programme *Desert Island Discs*, and I have been tempted to wonder how I would choose my eight records if I were asked to appear. Well, that will never happen, but I am confronted with a similar dilemma in that I have been asked to base this series of reflections upon nine favourite hymns.

Where to start? I have a very eclectic taste, ranging from some real oldies right through to modern choruses. Added to that, I am interested in hymns from other parts of the world. In order to narrow the field, I have decided to focus on hymns I have known all my life, with one exception – and that is the last in the series (I will explain in due course). The hymn book at church throughout my childhood was *Hymns Ancient and Modern* (standard edition, 1924). I wonder how many of you also grew up with that book.

I love hymns and often used to refer to them in sermons. As a consequence, when I retired from parochial ministry, a dear member of the evensong congregation, a Roman Catholic, gave me a book called *Sweet Sounds of Zion*. It is the transcripts of a series of 28 Radio 4 programmes on hymns, made in the 1970s by John Betjeman.

Betjeman's opening words were, 'Hymns are the poems of the people... they provide us with memories of happier, more devout days of Sunday school and school assemblies, of weddings and funerals. They have given phrases to our language.' Betjeman went further: he considered hymns to be at the forefront of literature and to be of considerable social importance.

In the years since Betjeman said that, the place of the church in society has changed dramatically, and I am not sure that the notion of 'the poems of the people' still holds. But for those of us who are part of church life, hymns are still special. They are an important part of our worship; they are full of devotional treasures, and in some cases they encapsulate both scriptural and theological truths and have considerable teaching value.

So here are a few of my 'Desert Island Hymns'!

GEOFF LOWSON

The day thou gavest, Lord, is ended

Now the eleven disciples went to Galilee, to the mountain to which Jesus had directed them. When they saw him, they worshipped him; but some doubted. And Jesus came and said to them, 'All authority in heaven and on earth has been given to me. Go therefore and make disciples of all nations, baptising them in the name of the Father and of the Son and of the Holy Spirit, and teaching them to obey everything that I have commanded you. And remember, I am with you always, to the end of the age.'

This hymn, with words by John Ellerton (1826–93), is consistently in the UK's top ten favourite hymns, according to the BBC. It is certainly a favourite of mine, but it is further etched upon my mind because, as a teenager, we had a vicar who was unwell and seemed to find comfort in singing this every Sunday evening.

The hymn directs our thoughts to the missionary endeavour of the church in fulfilling Jesus' instruction to 'go therefore and make disciples of all nations'. It reminds us that this work is never done and we must continue to strive, so that 'hour by hour fresh lips are making thy wondrous doings heard on high'. It also draws attention to the fact that the church is a worldwide community. As the world rotates, there is always someone in that fellowship offering worship, someone praying, someone preaching the gospel, someone keeping watch.

Sadly, but perhaps justifiably, the hymn comes in for some criticism. It was written in 1870 and was a great favourite of Queen Victoria, so it has been linked with British imperialism. But the final verse takes account of that, proclaiming that 'earth's proud empires pass away' but 'thy kingdom stands and grows forever'.

Jesus' instruction was to make disciples, to baptise and to teach. But very importantly that injunction was based upon 'everything that I have commanded you'. In other words, Jesus taught of a kingdom which is not about empire or earthly power but which is a foretaste of heaven.

May we join our prayers, our praise and our proclamation of the gospel of justice and peace with those of fellow Christians around the world.

GEOFF LOWSON

Eternal Father, strong to save

Some went down to the sea in ships, doing business on the mighty waters; they saw the deeds of the Lord, his wondrous works in the deep. For he commanded and raised the stormy wind, which lifted up the waves of the sea. They mounted up to heaven, they went down to the depths; their courage melted away in their calamity; they reeled and staggered like drunkards, and were at their wits' end. Then they cried to the Lord in their trouble, and he brought them out from their distress.

On two occasions I lived and worked by the sea, at the mouths of rivers, in towns famed for both shipbuilding and fishing. Those with deep roots in the communities had the sea in their blood; there was a great love of the sea, but huge respect for it too. Today's hymn takes on a deeper meaning when sung at the funeral of a fisherman or seafarer: 'Eternal Father, strong to save, whose arm does bind the restless wave, who bids the mighty ocean deep, its own appointed limits keep; O hear us when we cry to Thee, for those in peril on the sea' (William Whiting, 1860).

Psalm 107 praises the steadfast or loyal love of the Lord towards those in distress. It draws attention to four groups suffering hardship but who can depend upon God: those lost in the desert; those in the darkness of captivity; those in need of healing; and, today's passage, seafarers. The four groups can be scenes from life today, real or metaphorical, but they also represent Israel's experiences.

The Hebrew word used for this loyal love is *hesed*. It is important to note that it is an active word, not so much about feeling as doing, and in the psalm the writer refers to God's actions of *hesed* as 'wondrous works'.

In the lovely story of Ruth, we see *hesed* in Ruth's love for Naomi and in Boaz's support of Ruth. Used in this way, we are reminded that the quality of *hesed* is not restricted to God – those who love God must display it too.

'O give thanks to the Lord, for he is good; for his steadfast love [hesed] endures forever' (Psalm 107:1).

GEOFF LOWSON

We love the place, O God

[Solomon said:] 'I have built you an exalted house, a place for you to dwell in forever… But will God indeed dwell on the earth? Even heaven and the highest heaven cannot contain you, much less this house that I have built! Have regard to your servant's prayer and his plea, O Lord my God, heeding the cry and the prayer that your servant prays to you today; that your eyes may be open night and day towards this house, the place of which you said, "My name shall be there", that you may heed the prayer that your servant prays towards this place.'

For many readers, your church or chapel will be very special – a place you love and where you feel a closeness to God. 'We love the place, O God, wherein thine honour dwells; the joy of thine abode all earthly joy excels' (William Bullock, 1854). Today's passage is about Solomon's temple in Jerusalem. It was started in 966BC and took seven years to build. No remains of it have been discovered, but 1 Kings 6—7 describe it with such loving detail that one can visualise it. It must have been magnificent, a fit dwelling place for God.

But the writer of Kings raises an issue that still challenges us today. It concerns that tension between, on the one hand, loving our church building and encouraging people to come along to worship and, on the other hand, teaching that God is not contained within the walls.

The temple was the religious focus for the people of Israel but, importantly, it was also of huge cultural significance. There is an interesting parallel here – any clergy person can tell tales of people in the community referring to 'my church' who yet never cross the threshold. Because of our cultural inheritance, there is a residual 'feeling' for the building.

Our church may be an important focus for our faith, but it may have a deeper significance too. We need to 'heed the prayer that your servant prays towards this place'.

Reflect upon today's hymn as it speaks of the life of the church building: a place of prayer, teaching, the sacraments, worship and anticipation of things to come.

GEOFF LOWSON

Jesus, the very thought of thee

People were bringing little children to [Jesus] in order that he might touch them; and the disciples spoke sternly to them. But when Jesus saw this, he was indignant and said to them, 'Let the little children come to me; do not stop them; for it is to such as these that the kingdom of God belongs. Truly I tell you, whoever does not receive the kingdom of God as a little child will never enter it.' And he took them up in his arms, laid his hands on them, and blessed them.

Today's hymn is traditionally ascribed to Bernard of Clairvaux (1090–1153), and it focuses on the name, the love and the presence of Jesus. It describes a closeness, even intimacy, with our Lord – full of both gentleness and joy: 'Jesus, the very thought of thee with sweetness fills the breast; but sweeter far thy face to see, and in thy presence rest.' Today's passage from Mark is full of those same sentiments.

Behind the altar in the cathedral in Copenhagen there is a life-size statue of Christ by Bertel Thorvaldsen (1770–1844), which has a beautiful story associated with it. When Thorvaldsen made the original draft in clay, Christ's head was held high and thrown back, and he had strong arms outstretched and lifted up. It was a powerful, majestic Christ. Thorvaldsen went away for a few days, and on his return he opened the door to his studio only to stare in disbelief. There had been a weekend of thunderstorms and humidity, and the clay figure had sagged. The proud head was now bowed slightly towards the ground; the powerful outstretched arms had drooped. Thorvaldsen left the studio distraught and bewildered. Later that day he returned with a friend, and the friend, far from being appalled, was overwhelmed. He saw a gentle, compassionate Jesus with arms reaching out to welcome and embrace and a head lowered in compassion.

That is what I imagine whenever I sing this hymn or visualise the children running towards Jesus, rather like running to a favourite uncle.

Reflect upon any occasion in your life when disappointment,
or something apparently negative, has become a moment of revelation.

GEOFF LOWSON

I heard the voice of Jesus say

Jesus said to her, 'Everyone who drinks of this water will be thirsty again, but those who drink of the water that I will give them will never be thirsty. The water that I will give will become in them a spring of water gushing up to eternal life.' The woman said to him, 'Sir, give me this water, so that I may never be thirsty or have to keep coming here to draw water.'

I could easily have based my whole selection of hymns upon my favourite hymn composer of the day, Revd J.B. Dykes (1823–76). He spent most of his ministry at St Oswald's, Durham, and incredibly 60 of the tunes in the 1924 edition of *Hymns Ancient and Modern* are his.

This hymn has three verses, each of which begins with an invitation from Jesus followed by a response from the listener. The second verse relates to today's passage: 'I heard the voice of Jesus say, "Behold, I freely give the living water: thirsty one, stoop down, and drink, and live." I came to Jesus, and I drank of that life-giving stream. My thirst was quenched, my soul revived, and now I live in him.'

The Dykes tune to this hymn (Vox Dilecti) is unusual in that it changes key halfway through: the challenge from Jesus is in G minor and the positive response shifts to G major. It is a beautiful tune and a clever one! Any challenge from Jesus, or indeed any challenge from our faith, requires some sort of response and often that requires a shift of key.

Today's passage tells the concluding part of the encounter between Jesus and a Samaritan woman at a well. The woman is taken aback and confused that Jesus should ask for her help. As we see, Jesus offers her (and by implication us) the opportunity of 'living water'. One can sense the positive mood in the woman's response – one can hear the change of key from minor to major. Her questioning and confusion are replaced by optimism and vigour.

Well water is static and perhaps even stale. 'Gushing' water is dynamic and full of life. Is your faith like a well or a stream?

GEOFF LOWSON

All people that on earth do dwell

O be joyful in the Lord, all ye lands: serve the Lord with gladness, and come before his presence with a song. Be ye sure that the Lord he is God: it is he that hath made us, and not we ourselves; we are his people, and the sheep of his pasture. O go your way into his gates with thanksgiving, and into his courts with praise: be thankful unto him, and speak good of his Name. For the Lord is gracious, his mercy is everlasting: and his truth endureth from generation to generation.

It is a wonderful coincidence (or perhaps the editor planned it) that the church remembers Augustine of Hippo today. Why? One of the earliest and most celebrated definitions of a hymn comes from his pen. It is too wordy to quote in full, but here is part of it: 'A hymn is the praise of God by singing. For it to be a hymn it is needful for it to have three things: praise, praise of God and these sung.'

Psalm 100 was used liturgically; it was a processional song, probably used as people moved through the gates of the temple into its inner courts to worship. To the Israelites, moving 'into his courts' was actually moving into the presence of God. But the psalm is also theological, in that it spells out some of the elements of worship: joyfulness, service, gladness, thanksgiving, praise, awe of God and understanding.

Today's hymn is a wonderful paraphrase of Psalm 100, picking up on both the duty and the need within us to worship God: 'O enter then his gates with praise, approach with joy his courts unto: Praise, laud and bless his name always, for it is seemly so to do' (William Kethe, 1560).

We often begin our services with a hymn and a 'gathering' – that symbolic moving into the presence of God. It may be marked by a procession and ceremony, but, importantly, it is about focusing upon the kingdom of God.

In Jerusalem there were two buildings side by side: the palace of the human king and the temple of the divine King. The question in Israel's history was often, which really rules? Metaphorically, we are faced with the same question.

GEOFF LOWSON

O Jesus, I have promised

'I will not leave you orphaned; I am coming to you. In a little while the world will no longer see me, but you will see me; because I live, you also will live. On that day you will know that I am in my Father, and you in me, and I in you. They who have my commandments and keep them are those who love me; and those who love me will be loved by my Father, and I will love them and reveal myself to them.'

There are two cathedrals in Edinburgh. St Giles is probably better known because of its central position on the Royal Mile, but a little to the west of the city centre is St Mary's Episcopal Cathedral. In the north choir aisle of St Mary's there is a painting by A.E. Borthwick called *The Presence*.

The painting depicts a scene inside the cathedral itself. Imagine looking from the back: in the distance the sanctuary is bathed in light as the Eucharist is being celebrated. But at the back of the building we see a woman on her knees, clearly in some distress. Standing behind her is Jesus with his hand stretched out to comfort.

There is much to discuss in the picture, not least the juxtaposition of the presence of Christ in the Eucharist and his presence beside the woman. Then add to that the notion of Christ within us as described in today's passage from John.

Today's hymn was written by Revd John Bode in 1866 for his own children's confirmation service. The hymn is about commitment; it is about promises made and the challenge of keeping those promises in a hostile world. Importantly, though, it is about the assurance of the Lord's unfailing presence to help us when we feel we are failing.

In our passage, the disciples have reached a difficult time. They are struggling and wondering whether they can fulfil their commitments. Jesus assures them that they will not be left stranded because they can be sure of his presence both beside them and within them. That promise is extended to us too.

'O Jesus, I have promised to serve thee to the end;
be thou forever near me, my master and my friend.'

GEOFF LOWSON

Daisies are our silver

Consider how the lilies grow in the fields; they do not work, they do not spin; and yet, I tell you, even Solomon in all his splendour was not attired like one of these. But if that is how God clothes the grass in the fields, which is there today, and tomorrow is thrown on the stove, will he not all the more clothe you?... No, do not ask anxiously, 'What are we to eat? What are we to drink? What shall we wear?' All these are things for the heathen to run after, not for you, because your heavenly Father knows that you need them all. Set your mind on God's kingdom and his justice before everything else, and all the rest will come to you as well.

I was fortunate in having a happy, uncomplicated childhood. Church life was busy and committed but did not really challenge. I suspect that was the case for most rural and suburban parishes of the time. Today's hymn was in a blue book called *Songs of Praise* and has stayed with me since schooldays: 'Daisies are our silver, buttercups our gold. This is all the treasure we can have or hold' (Jan Struther, 1931).

It paints a delightfully innocent picture of the world and in so doing dovetails with my faith and church life from that time. But should our faith and church life be cosy? A dear South African friend of mine coined the terms 'duvet theology' and 'duvet church'! All very comfortable.

Of course, the church is there to offer comfort; indeed, I believe that pastoral work is very closely linked to mission. But it must also challenge. The passage from Matthew brings the two together. It paints a lovely picture of the world – the lilies of the field and so on – reminding us that God is in charge and that he has only good purposes for us. However, the passage also contains a challenge – the kingdom is both now and not yet, and we still have a part to play in ushering in God's justice for the world.

Reflect upon how your understanding of the gospel has evolved over the years.

GEOFF LOWSON

O Lord, all the world belongs to you

While they were searching for Paul and Silas to bring them out to the assembly, they attacked Jason's house. When they could not find them, they dragged Jason and some believers before the city authorities, shouting, 'These people who have been turning the world upside down have come here also, and Jason has entertained them as guests. They are all acting contrary to the decrees of the emperor, saying that there is another king named Jesus.' The people and the city officials were disturbed when they heard this, and after they had taken bail from Jason and the others, they let them go.

Paul is on his second missionary journey, with Silas. They have crossed over from what is now Turkey into Greece and travelled through Neapolis, Philippi and then to Thessalonica. Here, Paul's teaching upsets the establishment, who, as a result, hire a mob to track him down. Paul is accused of 'turning the world upside down' by his teaching.

I left school in 1965 to go to university. Inevitably I was exposed to all sorts of new and exciting ideas, including those that influenced my faith. There was new liturgy (who remembers Series 2 Communion in 1966?), new music and, of course, new theology. All of that led me to realise that our faith is not about being 'cosy' (see yesterday's reflection) but is about transformation, and that sometimes means turning things upside down.

Patrick Appleford was an Anglican priest who wrote this hymn in 1965 while working for the mission agency United Society Partners in the Gospel; it was the sort of new thinking that enthused me then, and it still excites me now: 'O Lord, all the world belongs to you, and you are always making all things new. Send your Spirit on all in your church whom you call to be turning the world upside down.'

The book of Acts tells the story of a handful of men and women who, by the power of the Holy Spirit, did not leave their world the same way they found it. They were ordinary people whom God enabled to do extraordinary things. We can still play our part.

Ponder this: in answer to the exam question 'What is the last book in the Bible?', a student wrote 'The book of Revolution'.

GEOFF LOWSON

This page is left blank for your notes

Overleaf… Reading *New Daylight* in a group | Author profile | Recommended reading | Order and subscription forms

Reading *New Daylight* in a group

SALLY WELCH

I am aware that although some of you cherish the moments of quiet during the day which enable you to read and reflect on the passages we offer you in *New Daylight*, other readers prefer to study in small groups, to enable conversation and discussion and the sharing of insights. With this in mind, here are some ideas for discussion starters within a study group. Some of the questions are generic and can be applied to any set of contributions within this issue; others are specific to certain sets of readings. I hope they generate some interesting reflections and conversations!

General discussion starters

These can be used for any study series within this issue. Remember there are no right or wrong answers – these questions are simply to enable a group to engage in conversation.

- What do you think the main idea or theme of the author in this series? Do you think they succeeded in communicating this to you, or were you more interested in the side issues?

- Have you had any experience of the issues that are raised in the study? How have they affected your life?

- What evidence does the author use to support their ideas? Do they use personal observations and experience, facts, quotations from other authorities? Which appeals to you most?

- Does the author make a 'call to action'? Is that call realistic and achievable? Do you think their ideas will work in the secular world?

- Can you identify specific passages that struck you personally – as interesting, profound, difficult to understand or illuminating?

- Did you learn something new reading this series? Will you think differently about some things, and if so, what are they?

Questions for specific series

Bethlehem and Nazareth – Liz Hoare

Liz begins her reflections with the statement that 'Geography shapes human life'. How has your life been shaped by the places you have lived? In what ways might Jesus' ministry have been different had he lived where you did? Jesus reached out to the poor and marginalised of his country – who are the 'poor and marginalised' where you live? How might you and your church reach out to them?

A pilgrim heart – Sally Welch

What do you think of the idea that the strangers we meet are like 'parcels in a Christmas stocking' – full of surprises? Who have you met recently who has confounded your expectations and in what ways? Is a pilgrim heart worth cultivating? What changes could you make in your life so that you 'make an adventure out of the everyday'?

Geoff Lowson's favourite hymn reminds him of his 'happy, uncomplicated' childhood, but he also warns of the dangers of a faith which is too comfortable and undemanding. What do you think are the advantages and disadvantages of 'duvet church'?

'Daisies are our silver,
Buttercups our gold:
This is all the treasure
we can have or hold'.
(Jan Struther, 1931)

New author interview: Ross Moughtin

How did you get from international runner to Liverpool vicar?

Strangely, from the top five 800m runners of my era, three of us went on to be ordained. I think I knew then that God was lining me up for ordained ministry and so I did my best to seek alternative employment, first as a journalist, then as a social worker and finally as an economist. The turning point came when I was – you won't believe this – interviewed by mistake at a theological college. When totally unexpectedly I was offered a place, I knew God had cornered me! Four months later I was on the course as a Liverpool ordinand.

Twenty-six years in one parish – what were the advantages and disadvantages of staying in the same place for so long?

Had I known I was going to stay at Christ Church for 26 years, we would have bought better carpets. We embarked on an ambitious and entirely necessary building project of a ministry centre, which took us 18 hard years. My main role was to maintain the momentum, sometimes against fierce opposition. I'm sure that my background as a 800m runner helped us to stay the course. However, the problem with 26 years of parish ministry in a market town is that everyone knows you. Complete strangers regularly come up to me and say, 'Hello, Ross! How's it going?'

Fifty Alpha courses – how did these change over the years?

Not very much. That, I think, was the secret as those who came to faith through each course invited their friends and relatives to the next. They knew what to expect, not least an encounter with God. Again the secret was in perseverance: some courses proved remarkably fruitful, others were disappointing. We kept at it.

What is your prognosis for the future of the Church of England?

We will always be in crisis. As a vicar, I would pray, 'Lord, this is your church, your responsibility. What do you want me to do?' Our only hope is God's faithfulness. I'm encouraged that this confidence is encouraging us to take risks, seeking new ways of sharing the good news of Jesus.

Your favourite book, film and meal?

Joseph Heller's *Catch-22*; *Chariots of Fire*; and I love bread, especially Turkish bread.

Recommended reading

How to read the Bible? And how to apply it? To read and engage with the Bible, we first need to understand the story, the styles of writing and the approaches we find in the text. Michael Parsons encourages readers to look at the whole biblical storyline before demonstrating ways of approaching individual texts. Topics along the way include understanding different genres, the importance of narrative, imaginative reading, praying the Bible, difficult passages and what to do with them, and how to apply scripture to our own lives.

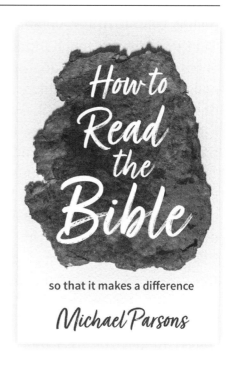

so that it makes a difference

Michael Parsons

The following is an edited extract from the chapter 'Why do we read the Bible?'

For some years now, I've read the Bible every twelve months or so. Beginning with the Psalms, I read the rest in a certain order, in lengthy portions, getting to know what the book is about. This, in itself, is useful, of course. However, this is what Eugene Peterson would term 'reading', not 'listening'. It's a good thing to do, but, as we've seen, it won't gain the desired purpose of scripture, which is for us to become mature in Christ, to know him in resurrection power and in suffering. To listen, I need to pause and contemplate the text, to pray through it, to reflect on the experience of God – Israel's or the writer's and my own – seeking to see the words as enculturated in the period of their composition, but somehow, through the wonderful present work of the Holy Spirit, applied to my own time and situation. To listen to scripture, I need to grasp something of the central importance of Jesus Christ to the narrative and to my own life and well-being. And, I would say, I need to grasp the importance of experiencing God through the Spirit as he informs my thinking and forms my life to exhibit something of Christ himself. It happens on a different level than merely reading scripture; it is 'listening to', or 'engaging with', scripture.

In his later work on the subject, *Eat This Book*, Eugene Peterson speaks of God revealing himself to us through the text of scripture as we 'listen', pulling us into the revelation and welcoming us as participants in it: 'God's word is written, handed down, and translated for us so that we can enter the plot.' This is an important point. It perhaps reminds us of the active word in Peter Phillips' image of the Bible as an engine – an engine driving us to recognise the God behind the words. But Peterson is speaking about the narrative of scripture, the story of God's people throughout biblical history (Old Testament and New), into which we are drawn by God's revelation to us through the witness of scripture. It reminds me of a fascinating study of tradition by Delwin Brown. Speaking of the curatorial character of tradition, he says it has force; it's experienced as some kind of distinctive pull. Employing an image, Brown speaks of it as more like a galaxy than a planet. The planet, he says, is static in its 'brute given-ness'; the galaxy, in contrast, functionally exerts its own gravitational pull, 'a kind of inner drive', with its ragged edges and its inner swirl. This seems reminiscent of much of what Peterson says about biblical narrative. If we 'listen' to it, it pulls us in, it has its own gravitational pull, 'a kind of inner drive'. And, as we enter the narrative of scripture, we work out who we are, our roots; we negotiate our own identity – it's a very personal thing.

It's a personal experience because it involves primarily the God of revelation and us, those who listen to or engage with his compelling voice. Eugene Peterson helpfully puts it this way:

> *But here's the thing: every aspect, every form is personal – God is relational at the core – and so whatever is said, whatever is revealed, whatever is received is also personal and relational… The corollary to this is that I, because I am a person, am personally involved in the revelation. Every word I hear, everything I see in my imagination as the story unfolds, involves me relationally, pulls me into participation, matters to my core identity, affects who I am and what I do.*

Why read the Bible? Because in reading, or rather 'listening', to use Peterson's helpful distinction, we listen for God's voice, his revelation to which the Bible is a faithful witness. We do so, of course, through other people's experiences of God and his salvation, and sometimes through their experiences of God's apparent absence. So, it's not always going to be easy reading/listening! Indeed, at times it is difficult to glean the Lord's voice at all. But we read in the hope and the confidence that because he is personal, his purpose for us is good. We read so that we might enter the storyline or narrative plot and be transformed little by little into the image of his precious son. We need to keep this in mind as we turn later to some strategies for reading the pages of scripture; we don't want to learn to read only to miss the divine art and purpose of listening.

*To order a copy of this book, please use the order form on page 149 or visit **brfonline.org.uk**.*

Really Useful Guides

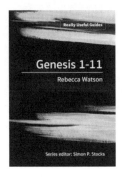  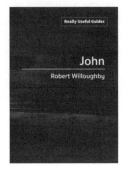 

Each Really Useful Guide focuses on a specific biblical book, making it come to life for the reader, enabling them to understand the message and to apply its truth to today's circumstances. Though not a commentary, it gives valuable insight into the book's message. Though not an introduction, it summarises the important aspects of the book to aid reading and application.

Genesis 1—11
Rebecca Watson
978 0 85746 791 1 £5.99

Psalms
Simon P. Stocks
978 0 85746 731 7 £6.99

John
Robert Willoughby
978 0 85746 751 5 £5.99

Colossians and Philemon
Derek Tidball
978 0 85746 730 0 £5.99

brfonline.org.uk

To order

Online: **brfonline.org.uk**
Telephone: +44 (0)1865 319700
Mon–Fri 9.15–17.30

Delivery times within the UK are normally 15 working days. Prices are correct at the time of going to press but may change without prior notice.

Title	Price	Qty	Total
How to Read the Bible	£8.99		
Really Useful Guides: Genesis 1–11	£5.99		
Really Useful Guides: John	£5.99		
Really Useful Guides: Colossians and Philemon	£5.99		
Really Useful Guides: Psalms	£6.99		

POSTAGE AND PACKING CHARGES			
Order value	UK	Europe	Rest of world
Under £7.00	£2.00	Available on request	Available on request
£7.00–£29.99	£3.00		
£30.00 and over	FREE		

Total value of books	
Postage and packing	
Total for this order	

Please complete in BLOCK CAPITALS

Title .... First name/initials .... Surname ....

Address ....

.... Postcode ....

Acc. No. .... Telephone ....

Email ....

Method of payment

❑ Cheque (made payable to BRF) ❑ MasterCard / Visa

Card no. ☐☐☐☐ ☐☐☐☐ ☐☐☐☐ ☐☐☐☐

Expires end ☐☐ ☐☐ Security code* ☐☐☐ Last 3 digits on the reverse of the card

Signature* .... Date .... / .... / ....
*ESSENTIAL IN ORDER TO PROCESS YOUR ORDER

Please return this form to:
BRF, 15 The Chambers, Vineyard, Abingdon OX14 3FE | **enquiries@brf.org.uk**
To read our terms and find out about cancelling your order, please visit **brfonline.org.uk/terms**.

BRF needs you!

If you're one of our many thousands of regular *New Daylight* readers, you will know all about the benefits and blessings of regular Bible reading and the value of daily notes to guide, inform and inspire you.

Here are some recent comments from *New Daylight* readers:

'Thank you for all the many inspiring writings that help so much when things are tough.'

'Just right for me – I learned a lot!'

'We looked forward to each day's message as we pondered each passage and comment.'

If you have similarly positive things to say about *New Daylight*, would you be willing to share your experience with others? Could you ask for a brief slot during church notices or write a short piece for your church magazine or website? Do you belong to groups, formal or informal, where you could share your experience of using Bible reading notes and encourage others to try them?

It doesn't need to be complicated or nerve-wracking: just answering these three questions in what you say or write will get your message across:

- How do Bible reading notes help you grow in your faith?
- Where, when and how do you use them?
- What would you say to people who don't already use them?

We can supply further information if you need it and would love to hear about it if you do give a talk or write an article.

For more information:

- Email **enquiries@brf.org.uk**
- Telephone BRF on +44 (0)1865 319700 Mon–Fri 9.15–17.30
- Write to us at BRF, 15 The Chambers, Vineyard, Abingdon OX14 3FE

Enabling all ages to grow in faith

At BRF, we long for people of all ages to grow in faith and understanding of the Bible. That's what all our work as a charity is about.

- Our **Living Faith** range of resources helps Christians go deeper in their understanding of scripture, in prayer and in their walk with God. Our conferences and events bring people together to share this journey.

- We also want to make it easier for local churches to engage effectively in ministry and mission – by helping them bring new families into a growing relationship with God through **Messy Church** or by supporting churches as they nurture the spiritual life of older people through **Anna Chaplaincy**.

- Our **Holy Habits** resources help whole congregations grow together as disciples of Jesus, living out and sharing their faith.

- Our **Parenting for Faith** team coaches parents and others to raise God-connected children and teens, and enables churches to fully support them.

- We also offer a professional education service, **Barnabas in Schools**, giving primary schools confidence, expertise and opportunities for exploring Christianity in creative ways that engage all pupils.

Do you share our vision?

Though a significant proportion of BRF's funding is generated through our charitable activities, we are dependent on the generous support of individuals, churches and charitable trusts.

If you share our vision, would you help us to enable even more people of all ages to grow in faith? Your prayers and financial support are vital for the work that we do. You could:

- Support BRF's ministry with a regular donation;
- Support us with a one-off gift;
- Consider leaving a gift to BRF in your will (see page 152);
- Encourage your church to support BRF as part of your church's giving to home mission – perhaps focusing on a specific ministry or programme;
- Most important of all, support BRF with your prayers.

Donate at **brf.org.uk/donate** or use the form on pages 153–54.

Making an impact

If someone asked you who throughout history (excluding Jesus) has left the biggest impact, what would be your answer?

For some, it may be Albert Einstein, who is responsible for developing the theory of relativity, came up with the formula $E = mc^2$ and in 1921 received the Nobel Prize in Physics.

For those who love to read, it may be someone like Johannes Gutenberg who, in 1439, invented the printing press.

Or maybe the person who has left the biggest impact, in your opinion, is someone who is close to you, whose name isn't widely known but whose contribution to your life is valuable.

Here at BRF, we have many people who contribute in such a way. They are people whose names are not widely known, but to us they are heroes.

It is because of these heroes – their willingness to partner with us and their financial gift – that we can continue inspiring and equipping future generations to grow in faith. Through access to our notes, books and creative programmes, people are encountering Jesus and lives are being impacted.

If you would like to partner with us, and the time is ever right for you to remember a charity in your will, please remember BRF.

For further information about making a gift to BRF in your will, please visit **brf.org.uk/lastingdifference**, contact us at **+44 (0)1865 319700** or email **giving@brf.org.uk**.

Whatever you can do or give, we thank you for your support.

> Pray. Give. Get involved.
> **brf.org.uk**

I would like to make a gift to support BRF. Please use my gift for:

☐ BRF charity ☐ Barnabas in Schools ☐ Parenting for Faith

☐ Messy Church ☐ Anna Chaplaincy ☐ where it is most needed

Title	First name/initials	Surname

Address	
	Postcode

Email

Telephone

Signature	Date

giftaid it You can add an extra 25p to every £1 you give.

Please treat as Gift Aid donations all qualifying gifts of money made

☐ today, ☐ in the past four years, ☐ and in the future.

I am a UK taxpayer and understand that if I pay less Income Tax and/or Capital Gains Tax in the current tax year than the amount of Gift Aid claimed on all my donations, it is my responsibility to pay any difference.

☐ My donation does not qualify for Gift Aid.

Please notify BRF if you want to cancel this Gift Aid declaration, change your name or home address, or no longer pay sufficient tax on your income and/or capital gains.

Please complete other side of form ➡

Please return this form to:
BRF, 15 The Chambers, Vineyard, Abingdon OX14 3FE

BRF

The Bible Reading Fellowship is a Registered Charity (233280)

Regular giving

By Direct Debit: You can set up a Direct Debit quickly and easily at **brf.org.uk/donate**

By Standing Order: Please contact our Fundraising Administrator +44 (0)1865 319700 | **giving@brf.org.uk**

One-off donation

Please accept my gift of:

☐ £10 ☐ £50 ☐ £100 Other £ ⬜

by (*delete as appropriate*):

☐ Cheque/Charity Voucher payable to 'BRF'

☐ MasterCard/Visa/Debit card/Charity card

Name on card

Card no. ⬜⬜⬜⬜ ⬜⬜⬜⬜ ⬜⬜⬜⬜ ⬜⬜⬜⬜

Expires end ⬜⬜ ⬜⬜ Security code* ⬜⬜⬜

*Last 3 digits on the reverse of the card
ESSENTIAL IN ORDER TO PROCESS YOUR PAYMENT

Signature | Date

☐ I would like to leave a gift in my will to BRF.

For more information, visit **brf.org.uk/lastingdifference**

For help or advice regarding making a gift, please contact our Fundraising Administrator +44 (0)1865 319700

↰ Please complete other side of form

Please return this form to:
BRF, 15 The Chambers, Vineyard, Abingdon OX14 3FE

BRF

The Bible Reading Fellowship is a Registered Charity (233280)

NEW DAYLIGHT SUBSCRIPTION RATES

Please note our new subscription rates, current until 30 April 2021:

Individual subscriptions
covering 3 issues for under 5 copies, payable in advance
(including postage & packing):

	UK	Europe	Rest of world
New Daylight	£17.85	£25.80	£29.70
New Daylight 3-year subscription (9 issues) (not available for Deluxe)	£50.85	N/A	N/A
New Daylight Deluxe per set of 3 issues p.a.	£22.35	£32.55	£38.55

Group subscriptions
covering 3 issues for 5 copies or more, sent to one UK address (post free):

New Daylight	£14.10 per set of 3 issues p.a.
New Daylight Deluxe	£17.85 per set of 3 issues p.a.

Please note that the annual billing period for group subscriptions runs from 1 May to 30 April.

Overseas group subscription rates
Available on request. Please email **enquiries@brf.org.uk**.

Copies may also be obtained from Christian bookshops:

New Daylight	£4.70 per copy
New Daylight Deluxe	£5.95 per copy

All our Bible reading notes can be ordered online by visiting
brfonline.org.uk/collections/subscriptions

 New Daylight is also available as an app for Android, iPhone and iPad
brfonline.org.uk/collections/apps

NEW DAYLIGHT INDIVIDUAL SUBSCRIPTION FORM

All our Bible reading notes can be ordered online by visiting
brfonline.org.uk/collections/subscriptions

☐ I would like to take out a subscription:

Title _____ First name/initials _____ Surname _____

Address _____

_____ Postcode _____

Telephone _____ Email _____

Please send *New Daylight* beginning with the September 2020 / January 2021 / May 2021 issue (*delete as appropriate*):

(*please tick box*)	UK	Europe	Rest of world
New Daylight 1-year subscription	☐ £17.85	☐ £25.80	☐ £29.70
New Daylight 3-year subscription	☐ £50.85	N/A	N/A
New Daylight Deluxe	☐ £22.35	☐ £32.55	☐ £38.55

Total enclosed £ _____ (cheques should be made payable to 'BRF')

Please charge my MasterCard / Visa ☐ Debit card ☐ with £ _____

Card no. ☐☐☐☐ ☐☐☐☐ ☐☐☐☐ ☐☐☐☐

Expires end ☐☐ ☐☐ Security code* ☐☐☐ Last 3 digits on the reverse of the card

Signature* _____ Date _____ / _____ / _____

*ESSENTIAL IN ORDER TO PROCESS YOUR PAYMENT

To set up a Direct Debit, please also complete the Direct Debit instruction on page 159 and return it to BRF with this form.

Please return this form with the appropriate payment to:
BRF, 15 The Chambers, Vineyard, Abingdon OX14 3FE

To read our terms and find out about cancelling your order, please visit **brfonline.org.uk/terms**.

BRF

The Bible Reading Fellowship is a Registered Charity (233280)

ND0220

NEW DAYLIGHT GIFT SUBSCRIPTION FORM

☐ I would like to give a gift subscription (please provide both names and addresses):

Title _____ First name/initials _____ Surname _____

Address _____

_____ Postcode _____

Telephone _____ Email _____

Gift subscription name _____

Gift subscription address _____

_____ Postcode _____

Gift message (20 words max. or include your own gift card):

_____

_____

Please send *New Daylight* beginning with the September 2020 / January 2021 / May 2021 issue (*delete as appropriate*):

(*please tick box*)	UK	Europe	Rest of world
New Daylight 1-year subscription	☐ £17.85	☐ £25.80	☐ £29.70
New Daylight 3-year subscription	☐ £50.85	N/A	N/A
New Daylight Deluxe	☐ £22.35	☐ £32.55	☐ £38.55

Total enclosed £ _____ (cheques should be made payable to 'BRF')

Please charge my MasterCard / Visa ☐ Debit card ☐ with £ _____

Card no. ☐☐☐☐ ☐☐☐☐ ☐☐☐☐ ☐☐☐☐

Expires end ☐☐ ☐☐   Security code* ☐☐☐   Last 3 digits on the reverse of the card

Signature* _____ Date _____ /_____ /_____

*ESSENTIAL IN ORDER TO PROCESS YOUR PAYMENT

To set up a Direct Debit, please also complete the Direct Debit instruction on page 159 and return it to BRF with this form.

Please return this form with the appropriate payment to:
BRF, 15 The Chambers, Vineyard, Abingdon OX14 3FE

To read our terms and find out about cancelling your order, please visit **brfonline.org.uk/terms**.

The Bible Reading Fellowship is a Registered Charity (233280)

You can pay for your annual subscription to our Bible reading notes using Direct Debit. You need only give your bank details once, and the payment is made automatically every year until you cancel it. If you would like to pay by Direct Debit, please use the form opposite, entering your BRF account number under 'Reference number'.

You are fully covered by the Direct Debit Guarantee:

The Direct Debit Guarantee

- This Guarantee is offered by all banks and building societies that accept instructions to pay Direct Debits.

- If there are any changes to the amount, date or frequency of your Direct Debit, The Bible Reading Fellowship will notify you 10 working days in advance of your account being debited or as otherwise agreed. If you request The Bible Reading Fellowship to collect a payment, confirmation of the amount and date will be given to you at the time of the request.

- If an error is made in the payment of your Direct Debit, by The Bible Reading Fellowship or your bank or building society, you are entitled to a full and immediate refund of the amount paid from your bank or building society.

- If you receive a refund you are not entitled to, you must pay it back when The Bible Reading Fellowship asks you to.

- You can cancel a Direct Debit at any time by simply contacting your bank or building society. Written confirmation may be required. Please also notify us.

The Bible Reading Fellowship

Instruction to your bank or building society to pay by Direct Debit

Please fill in the whole form using a ballpoint pen and return it to:
BRF, 15 The Chambers, Vineyard, Abingdon OX14 3FE

Service User Number: | 5 | 5 | 8 | 2 | 2 | 9 |

Name and full postal address of your bank or building society

To: The Manager	Bank/Building Society
Address	
	Postcode

Name(s) of account holder(s)

Branch sort code

| | | – | | | – | | |

Bank/Building Society account number

| | | | | | | | |

Reference number

| | | | | | | | |

Instruction to your Bank/Building Society
Please pay The Bible Reading Fellowship Direct Debits from the account detailed in this instruction, subject to the safeguards assured by the Direct Debit Guarantee. I understand that this instruction may remain with The Bible Reading Fellowship and, if so, details will be passed electronically to my bank/ building society.

Signature(s)

Banks and Building Societies may not accept Direct Debit instructions for some types of account.

Enabling all ages to grow in faith

Anna Chaplaincy

Barnabas in Schools

Holy Habits

Living Faith

Messy Church

Parenting for Faith

The Bible Reading Fellowship (BRF) is a Christian charity that resources individuals and churches and provides a professional education service to primary schools.

Our vision is to enable people of all ages to grow in faith and understanding of the Bible and to see more lay people equipped to exercise their gifts in leadership and ministry.

To find out more about our work and activities, visit

brf.org.uk